Out
Survival

Garth Hattingh

First published in 2004 by New Holland Publishers Ltd
London • Cape Town • Sydney • Auckland
www.newhollandpublishers.com

86 Edgware Road
London
W2 2EA
United Kingdom

14 Aquatic Drive
Frenchs Forest
NSW 2086
Australia

80 McKenzie Street
Cape Town
8001
South Africa

218 Lake Road
Northcote
Auckland
New Zealand

ISBN 1 84330 587 9 (Paperback)

Publisher Mariëlle Renssen
Publishing Managers Claudia Dos Santos,
Simon Pooley
Senior Designer Geraldine Cupido
Editor Leizel Brown
Designer Janine Cloete
Illustrators Steven Felmore, Chip Snaddon
Picture Researcher Karla Kik
Production Myrna Collins

Reproduction by Hirt & Carter Cape (Pty) Ltd
Printed and bound in Singapore by Tien Wah Press (Pte) Ltd

2 4 6 8 10 9 7 5 3 1

Outdoor
Survival

CONTENTS

SURVIVAL
PRINCIPLES

The very nature of survival situations is that they often arise when one least expects them. Few people knowingly place themselves in positions where their very existence is at stake. However, the growth in adventure sports such as off-piste skiing, kayaking, climbing, mountaineering, back-country hiking, micro-light flying and sailing has meant that more people are suddenly finding themselves in life-and-death situations. A large number of recent survival incidents has involved backpackers, 4x4 enthusiasts, snowmobiles or small boats. It is fair to say that most survival situations have been unanticipated by the persons concerned, although this is not to say that they arose inevitably – human fallibility often has a good deal to do with it.

Ice climbing is one activity where preparation and training are paramount, as one misplaced footing could spell disaster. Besides the meticulous planning, correct equipment such as crampons, pickaxe and helmet is indispensable.

Before setting out on any hike, ensure that you are equipped with vital skills such as navigation and route finding.

AVOIDING SURVIVAL SITUATIONS

Perhaps the most self-evident aspect is to try to avoid getting into survival situations in the first place. There are unfortunate times when one can do absolutely nothing to prevent this – a commercial aeroplane crash, the wreck of a pleasure liner and entirely unpredictable natural disasters such as earthquakes, tornadoes, hurricanes or freak avalanches. However, many incidents arise because an individual or group is inadequately prepared for the area or the activity and is thus unable to cope with the conditions. An important consideration should always be 'Have I the right equipment for the task, and enough of it?' Equally important is to ask 'Do I have sufficient background and knowledge for the task?'

There is often no substitute for experience – this adage is frequently forgotten in the information overload of our modern, fast-paced world. Going deep into back-country woods on an adventure trip in the middle of winter is hardly a suitable activity for novice hikers – yet a surprising number of rookie groups do just this, often with sadly predictable and even fatal consequences.

This is not to say 'Stay at home, and never go hiking or exploring the outdoors.' Far from it – outdoors and adventure activities provide a magnificent escape from the stresses of everyday life, and can have great character-

is informed – they might end up being the ones who need the knowledge, or the only ones capable of using it. And if you are one of the younger members of your family, persuade your parents and older siblings to read this book.

It would most certainly do no harm to study and practise some of the principles covered on these pages, and it might make the difference between life and death. At the very least, it may enhance your experience of a recreational outdoor excursion.

A certain agility is needed to move across rocks or difficult terrain, so don't make the mistake of assuming that you don't need to be fit to hike.

building benefits. What is important, however, is to match the activity or the level of the activity to your experience and that of the group. To take a group of amateur climbers on an extreme climbing expedition in the Canadian Rockies would be courting disaster, no matter how experienced the leader may be. It may just be the leader who dies or is injured during the trip.

The focus of this book is to help outdoor adventurers be better equipped when things go radically wrong and survival is at stake. If you are a parent reading this, make sure that your family

Thorough research is the basis for a successful and well-organized adventure experience. Guide books are useful 'tools', and the Internet provides almost instant feedback on numerous locations worldwide.

THE ART OF SURVIVAL

Survival can call for some unusual or, perhaps, initially even offensive actions such as trapping animals, eating raw food and bunking down in extremely cramped conditions. The key is to be prepared to do 'whatever it takes' to stay alive. Although there is generally little room for the niceties of 21st-century civilization when you find yourself in a survival situation, one aspect should always stay firmly in place: that of cooperation with others. You cannot predict when and how you will need the support of your fellow survivors.

When planning your trip, plot several alternative routes in case of an emergency situation. It is important to refer to your map frequently to avoid getting lost.

Land – practical tips

- Climbing down a steep rock face is far more difficult than climbing up. Practise, particularly if you frequent steep mountainous areas. The most agile members of a group can help others with vital foot placements from below.
- Creating shelter, trapping, finding food, and moving through difficult and unfamiliar territory all require prior practice to be efficient. Cooperation and mutual assistance are necessary to succeed in a survival situation.
- Building shelter as soon as possible can have the added benefits of helping to attain emotional stability and giving a group something to keep them busy in the early stages after a disaster scenario. In very cold climates, hypothermia (low body temperature) can be an insidious killer.
- Be constantly aware of your surroundings – you will have useful information in the case of emergencies. Do not rely only on the 'group leader' or 'guide' to follow your group's progress on the map; ask to be shown where you are every time the map is consulted.
- Be sure to make a mental note of noticeable features like rivers, lakes, roads and buildings; and of caves and hollows as possible shelter.
- If you are stranded in an entirely unfamiliar area, following a calamity such as an air or train accident, send out one or more scouting parties to look for shelter, food and water as soon as it is feasible to do so without adding to the trauma of the situation.

Before you undertake any journey into the wilderness in your vehicle, check that it has a spare tyre, that you have the necessary tools to effect minor repairs, that the jack works, that you have snow chains and a shovel and that there is spare fuel, food and water. For a long drive in very cold country, ensure that there is warm clothing in the car – air conditioners and heaters are not much use when you are trapped in a blizzard. Work on the assumption that you might just have to overnight in the car – and pack accordingly.

On a hiking trip you should make regular stops, watch the lie of the land and know in which direction you are travelling.

Water – practical tips

- Always assume that things might go wrong even when undertaking a day trip out to sea or on a large lake. Pack some extra water and food in waterproof containers and take extra clothing to cope with storms and cold.

- Keeping the group together after an accident at sea or on a river may well save lives – a group can encourage its weakening members, while a 'survival huddle' can help to preserve warmth and keep members afloat.

- Check the craft thoroughly beforehand to make sure that it has signalling devices; that the motors, sails and lanyards are sound; that you have suffi-

cient fuel if it is a powerboat; that the bungs are in – leave nothing to chance.

- A raft or other flotation device will assist staying alive on water, be it in the sea or when attempting to travel down a tributary in the hope of reaching a major river with some river traffic.

- Strong, positive leadership is vital if you wish to initiate and maintain any cooperative formation in the group.

- Knowledge of ropes, basic knots and lashings is invaluable in creating a temporary flotation device.

- If it is not your own craft, be sure to ask pertinent safety questions. It is your life, and that of your friends or family.

In this survival huddle, an empty plastic container is used to aid flotation, enabling the group members to conserve energy.

Airfilled trousers help to keep this swimmer's head above water, saving precious energy resources.

TACTICS FOR SURVIVAL

A study of numerous survival incidents by the American Rescue Institute has identified certain characteristic common elements of individuals or groups who survive in contrast to those who do not. One of the key factors has been the familiar Boy Scouts' motto: 'Be prepared'. Those who have survived against the odds have not necessarily been the toughest physically, or had the correct equipment. The essence of true survivors has often been mental readiness to handle unexpected challenges in a survival situation.

There are many documented feats of incredible endurance – up to 45 days without any food, a week without water, surviving for several days in freezing conditions, epic perseverance in blazing sun. All these grim accounts bear testimony to the hardiness of the human spirit and to the tenacity of those who have clung to life at all costs. In many of these cases, some members of the group have simply given up and let death overtake them, whereas the will to survive has kept others going against all odds.

Survivors in desperate situations have often reported that one individual or in some cases, a few, had the unshakable optimism that they would be rescued or somehow manage to get themselves out of the situation. The importance of one's mental attitude cannot be overemphasized – the difference between life and death in a survival situation truly often lies 'in the mind'.

After 70 days of being stranded in the Andes mountains, these aeroplane crash survivors resorted to cannibalism.

Undertaking short hikes is one way of preparing for a more strenuous multi-day trip. With each hike, gradually work your way to more challenging terrain.

PREPAREDNESS
Physical preparedness

Although it is perhaps not the most important factor in survival, there is no doubt that a fit, healthy person has some advantages over someone who is less physically prepared. Knowingly going into areas where extreme situations might arise – challenging white water, high mountain wilderness or polar regions – without being physically fit is tantamount to idiocy.

- Exercise – aerobics, weight training, running, cycling, rowing, for example. If necessary, consult a reputable and experienced personal trainer or fitness consultant to work out a suitable training programme aimed at improving your general level of fitness and focus on any specialized fitness requirements you may need.

- Health basics – dental problems, a routine medical check-up, any nagging ailments, sprained muscles or ligament injuries – should all be taken care of before taking a long trip.

- Inoculations – where required these help prevent hepatitis A, tetanus, yellow fever, etc.; also purchase prophylactic medicines (i.e. anti-malarial drugs) before embarking on your trip.

SURVIVAL PRINCIPLES

Activity preparedness

Remember that each activity has certain skills that need to be honed. Don't hesitate to consult experts for coaching and advice before your trip.

- Trackless desert – extensive 4x4 driving courses and motor maintenance.
- Sea kayaking – expertise in handling waves, swells and currents.
- Climbing – knowledge of techniques and specialized equipment.

A flooded river is not the place to learn how to eskimo roll in a canoe, and fumbling with unfamiliar knots in a whiteout storm is not the wisest move when you are perched on a 6000m (20,000ft) peak.

Training to raise fitness levels before a trip is important and can be tailored to a specific routine.

A person who is physically fit has a definite advantage when faced with a survival situation out in the wilderness.

Mental preparedness

Of all the aspects of survival, the mind is probably the most important. People who have survived against all odds have been those who wanted to survive with every fibre of their being. Most creatures have this instinct for survival, but it is likely that only man can rationalize survival and consciously decide to give up or go on. The survivors are those who are mentally prepared to give their all and never give in. Mental toughness is what true survival is all about. Fight the doubts, fight the tendency to say 'I will never make it' – focus instead on the incredible survival records of others. If they did it, so can you.

A suitable map is essential when planning a trip. Its scale and detail will depend on the type of terrain in which you intend travelling.

Leadership

Any group has individuals with various strengths and weaknesses and is subject to a conflict of personalities that can rip the group apart and reduce the chances of survival. Firm but tactful leadership can be essential in tough survival situations, particularly in the initial stages after a disaster. If a natural competent leader does not emerge, it is wise for the group to democratically elect a 'captain' as soon as possible. It has been amply proven that even poor leadership under extreme conditions is better than no leadership at all.

Mountaineers on Mount Tarawera listen carefully to their leader's briefing.

QUALITIES OF AN IDEAL LEADER

- Is sensitive to group and individual needs, but able to exercise firm control over factors such as food and liquid rationing, allocation of space, clothing and equipment, medical priorities, restrictions on movement and distribution of tasks.
- Is able to make major decisions in consultation with the group to avoid anyone feeling left out or abandoned (and later becoming a problem due to this isolation, real or imagined).
- Is flexible, but not vacillating in any decision-making.
- Will be prepared to hand over leadership either permanently or temporarily under certain circumstances, for example in a medical emergency if one of the party has more medical knowledge, or if a colleague has better mountaineering skills and a steep cliff is encountered.
- Shows a confidence and optimism that he or she may not truly feel. Survival can be toughest on the leader.

A good leader is one who regularly communicates with the group and makes decisions that are in the best interest of all concerned.

Knowledge of survival strategies

Even with the absolute minimum of equipment, all is not lost. The knowledge of survival tricks and strategies and the will to survive are powerful tools. Simply reading guides such as this gives you an advantage in the survival stakes while any practice you may have undertaken strengthens your hand immeasurably. Perhaps the best survival strategy is the one that is often forgotten – STOP and THINK. A carefully worked out, logical solution is more likely to succeed than a spur-of-the-moment 'quick fix'.

KEY SURVIVAL PRINCIPLES

- **Be prepared** Preparedness may encompass several forms such as personal physical condition, equipment, activity, advance planning, mental preparedness, leadership factors and knowledge of survival strategies. (For details see pp14–17.)

- **Practise essential skills** Practice makes perfect – many difficult skills such as lashings, firemaking and navigation will not be of much value unless you practise them enough to be confident in using them. If you are insecure in their application under ideal conditions, how much worse is it going to be in a howling gale, with cold, hungry, injured party members depending on you? On their own, these constitute fun activities that can liven up a hiking trip or provide an entertaining afternoon in the comfort of your local woods next to your favourite fishing hole.

  Why not plan a family, club or scout troop survival weekend, complete with firemaking, building shelter, some navigation exercises and primitive fishing and food gathering (perhaps with a little emergency canned food hidden away in the car boot in case you need it)?

- **Assess the situation** Avoiding panic, pausing to evaluate the resources of the situation and the group, and examining your options are essential before adopting a course of action. Every survival situation is unique – there

Lashing is a useful skill that should be practised regularly before going on trips. The more confident you are about survival techniques under ideal circumstances, the better you will cope if stranded in a disaster situation.

will be a novel mix of people, a specific set of conditions, a different amount of equipment. However, there will usually be common threads running through all incidents, with optimal ways of solving problems. The normal skills of everyday modern life become largely meaningless, and decisions have to be made about unfamiliar circumstances. It becomes very difficult to predict the outcomes, and conventional logic often seems irrelevant.

- **Adapt or die** Clear thinking and an appraisal of the situation is needed. The ability to adapt methods and patterns to accommodate new and unusual circumstances becomes vital. The party or individual may have to adapt to new ideas on movement patterns, food, clothing, water use, independence and leadership, to name but a few.

  Modern urban man has lost touch with his natural environment and is generally ill-equipped to deal with the harsh realities of nature without his comfort zone of pre-prepared food, water on tap, convenience clothing and mechanical and electrical devices. Yet man is also a survivor by nature, and the basic instincts of 'fight or flight' are there to stand you in good stead if you can conquer your fear of the unknown long enough to use them.

  Evaluate every item and situation in a new way and questions need to be asked. How can I use this piece of equipment? Should I take it along or leave it behind? Of what benefit can this item be to me? Nothing should be taken for granted.

ADVANCE AND CONTINGENCY PLANNING

Information is another vital key – the more facts you have on the area, the better prepared you are for survival. Make a point of finding out about the people, their lifestyles, customs and taboos; anticipated weather patterns; heights and topography of hills and mountains; river flow; vegetation; edible and inedible plants; animal life; ocean currents and water temperatures. The Internet and books offer a wealth of information, as do travellers who have already visited a particular area. Be sure to take along up-to-date maps, guide books and books on fauna and flora. Carefully plan the entire trip with your group before leaving. Any delays or disasters will be so much easier to handle if the responsibility is shared and you can tap into your companions' knowledge.

Delegate responsibilities to different team members, such as food planning, route mapping, equipment collection and emergency contingencies. Decide beforehand who will be the quartermaster, the cook, the navigator, mechanic, medic and leader.

These roles should, however, be flexible. Each group member should be able to assume another role and responsibility as this will help spread the organizer's load. Ensure that each member leaves details such as the scheduling dates, list of participants and contact details with their next of kin in case of an emergency.

An organized expedition through acacia country in Mali, near Timbuktu. A convoy of similar vehicles will minimize the spares and tyres that have to be carried.

A wise leader involves the entire group in planning, as this will stand them in good stead should a serious situation arise in the wilderness. If everyone feels involved in crucial discussions, it makes the difficult decisions easier to accept.

Making contingency plans

Depending on the nature of the excursion, various advance contingency plans need to be put in place.

- Plan your schedule: For all trips, especially those in back country, the wilderness and at sea, have an expected departure and trip completion time and projected contact plan. If the scheduled contacts are not adhered to, your contact person(s) should be instructed to notify the relevant authorities and should be given clear instructions on what steps to take.
- Route plan: Leave your projected trip plan with a suitable official contact person or with relevant authorities such as forestry, mountain rescue, the harbour master, coastguard, or aviation control if you are undertaking a private flight of any nature.
- Emergency escape routes: If you are planning a long hike in mountains or an extended river trip, plot several emergency escape routes on the route card. Always leave a copy with your contact person. In the case of injury or other delays, this will help rescuers narrow their search options.
- Regrouping plan: If you are going hiking, skiing or canoeing in back-country areas, make clear plans both beforehand and on a daily or even hourly basis for regrouping or other action in case your group becomes separated or one of the members goes missing.

Commercial adventure operators

There are some excellent commercial operators with flawless records and impeccable operating procedures but others fly close to the wind and can put their group at risk. It is important to do thorough research on adventure operators before you consider using their services. If necessary, ask for recommendations from others who have used commercial operators. You could also ask the operator for references and the names of previous clients whom you could contact.

It is crucial to maintain a sense of calm when faced with hostile behaviour in politically tense circumstances.

WHAT TO LOOK FOR IN AN OPERATOR

You would not put your life in the hands of a doctor for a critical operation unless you had done some research on him – so place your adventure operator under the same scrutiny. Insist on being provided with pertinent information. Only when you are satisfied with the answers should you make use of any operator's services.

- What is their track record?
- How long has the company been operating?
- Is your proposed trip one that is regularly offered by the operator?
- Does the operator use only qualified and experienced guides?
- Does the operator carry public liability insurance? (This is a very good way of establishing an operator's solid track record, since only established companies can obtain and afford public liability under normal circumstances.)
- Which authority issued the operator's credentials – national body or similar?
- What is their equipment like? (Ask to see it if necessary.)
- Does the operator have contingency plans in the event of an emergency or accident? If so, ask them to specify.

COPING WITH HOSTILE BEHAVIOUR

- Avoid sudden hand movements, particularly into a bag, your vehicle or pockets – these could well be misinterpreted as an attempt to reach for a weapon.
- Make a submissive gesture, such as palms up, hands forward, head slightly bowed to symbolize 'I have no weapon, and am not a threat'.
- Avoid aggressive eye contact and any form of verbal argument or confrontation in a hostile situation.
- Avoid wearing expensive clothes or flashy jewellery and do not openly display money, pricey cameras and watches.
- If someone is determined to take your possessions, even after you have quietly but firmly refused, hand them over. Your life should always take precedence over material possessions.
- Respect local dress and cultural or religious codes of conduct (e.g. covering the head, women refraining from wearing shorts, not drinking in public).
- Waiting may constitute part of the process – impatience is noticed and seldom appreciated by those who deem themselves to be 'in charge'. This seems to be true of many passport authorities in particular – petty border-post officials like to wield a great deal of power in order to delay, confiscate your goods or even imprison you. It is best to cooperate in hostile encounters.
- Never shout and gesticulate. Rather be as calm, undemanding and friendly as the circumstances allow – you may survive a situation that might otherwise spiral out of your control.
- Do not take photographs of military installations, government buildings or security forces.
- Do not make, or respond positively towards, derogatory comments about the country's government, current leader or those in authority, even if you think that the locals may agree with you.
- Ensure that all legal medicines are properly boxed, with full and appropriate labelling. NEVER carry drugs and avoid carrying liquor, especially when travelling in a Muslim country.
- Carry a 'sacrificial bank roll' in an accessible pocket or pouch where it can be easily reached. Your main cash and travel documents should be carried hidden in a thin pouch under your clothing.

BASIC KIT

There are essentially two kinds of survival situations: those that occur without warning during an everyday activity – such as an aeroplane trip that turns into a disaster when it crashes in inaccessible terrain – and unintentional mishaps that occur when a person or group takes part in a planned outdoor activity. In the former, one is unlikely to be carrying any form of substantial survival kit; in the latter, where there is a likelihood of potential problems that may result in a survival situation, it is always wise to be well prepared by including certain basic survival items or an entire survival kit in your personal or group luggage. This could reduce or even avert a survival situation.

Careful forward planning needs to take into account the correct type of clothing and equipment to suit your chosen activity – never underestimate environmental conditions.

NORMAL HIKING KIT

Most multi-day hikes require a basic set of gear such as a sleeping bag and groundsheet (or a tent), clothing, eating utensils and food. It takes experience of several trips before you discover the optimal collection of hiking and camping gear. Even on day hikes, you should have items such as raincoats, water bottles, long trousers, a warm top, a first-aid kit, a lamp and some food. Having the correct equipment can reduce the impact of a potential survival situation.

PERSONAL KIT

- **Backpack** This is the first item in your personal kit. Choose your pack carefully from the wide selection available. A quality backpack should be appropriate to your body size, hold all the items you need to take along, and above all, be durable and comfortable. For any hike longer than a few hours' duration, it is vital to have a well-padded hip belt that helps to stabilize and hold the weight of your pack, thus relieving pressure on your shoulders.

Apart from normal hiking gear, each member of the group should also have the following equipment:

- **Head lamp** A compact but powerful head lamp makes travelling in bush or steep terrain safer. Take along spare batteries and bulbs. Make sure that the lamp cannot switch on accidentally and therefore deplete the batteries.
- **Raincoat** A good raincoat is essential and can provide insulation in cold or windy conditions. It is preferable to choose one with a drawstring-type hood. Some raincoats, made from high-quality 'breathable' fabric, keep you drier than standard plastic raincoats because they allow perspiration to pass through.
- **Water bottle** Even in areas with good water supplies, it is always wise to carry a full bottle – particularly if the water you find might have to be purified before use.
- **Warm clothing** Do not be caught unprepared by changing weather conditions. Tracksuit pants, a warm top and a balaclava are advised for most hikes.

BIG SURVIVAL POUCH

EXTRA ACTIVITY SPECIFIC KIT

GROUP KIT

MINI SURVIVAL KIT

MEDICAL KIT

NORMAL HIKING KIT

A well-organized method of packing the compartments of a backpack ensures easy accessibility.

HEAD LAMP

WATER BOTTLES

RAINCOAT

WARM JACKET

NORMAL HIKING KIT

SURVIVAL POUCH

On hikes or multi-day trips a larger survival pouch on your backpack would usually contain a mini survival kit. The survival items in this kit can fit into a small tin or other waterproof container that can be easily carried in a pocket or pouchbag when embarking on an adventure into the wilderness. For frequent aeroplane travellers who pride themselves on always being prepared, a mini survival kit could easily fit into a jacket or briefcase side pocket. Many hunters and fishermen like to pack the items into their many-pocketed vests.

PERSONAL MINI SURVIVAL KIT

- **Plastic bag** Choose a strong one to carry or to collect water in a still.
- **Flexible (wire) saw** This is useful as it can even cut large branches. Coat with grease and keep in a plastic bag.
- **Surgical blade** For cutting off dead skin or a multitude of other uses.
- **Fish hooks** Choose ones that are intended for small- to medium-sized fish (e.g. gauge 5). Include a few small, pea-sized sinkers.
- **Wire** Thin wire (e.g. brass picture wire) is useful for making snares and many other tasks such as fixing shoes.
- **Button compass** Buy one that is preferably luminous and check on it regularly as small compasses are prone to rust.
- **Candle** This is used to start a fire rather than as a light source.
- **Magnifying glass** Vital for starting tinder fires or it can be used to make splinter removal easier.
- **Safety pins** These perform various fastening functions and can also double as fish hooks.
- **Waterproof matches** These are either bought as such, or standard matches can be waterproofed by dipping them in hot candle wax.
- **Flint** This often has a magnesium block with it to aid fire lighting. Shavings from the block usually flare up easily when lit.
- **Butterfly sutures** Invaluable for holding a wound together.
- **Needle and thread** Used to repair clothes, sleeping bags, etc.
- **Plasters** Preferably waterproof and in many different sizes.

A mini survival kit, which includes a mini medical kit, can be fitted into a small, robust tin.

Mini medical kit

This kit should comprise basic medical supplies and some clearly labelled basic tablets packaged in plastic.

- **Analgesic:** (e.g. Paracetamol – Acetaminophen in the USA) and/or codeine phosphate.
- **Anti-diarrhoea medication:** e.g. Loperamide (Immodium®).
- **Antihistamine:** e.g. Promethazine (Phenergan®) – for insect bites, stings, allergies, etc.
- **Latex gloves:** crepe bandage and a sterile wound dressing.

This little pouch can be kept in a separate, bigger survival bag.

SURVIVAL KIT FOR GROUPS

Besides each person having his/her own kit, there should also be group items.

- **Compass:** A good compass preferably one with a luminous dial (e.g. the Silva-type or Polaris compass).
- **Maps:** A reliable topographical map (to a scale of 1:50,000 or more detailed) should be laminated or carried in a waterproof pouch.
- **Stove and fuel:** Gas stoves with detachable cartridges are generally the safest. Use propane-butane fuel for higher altitudes.

Detachable compact gas burner; multi-fuel stove; detachable high-output gas burner.

- **Water purification tablets:** To purify natural water before use. Remember that few water sources are unpolluted.
- **First-aid kit:** This should include plasters, bandages, antiseptic cream, scissors, forceps, latex gloves and certain basic medicines (see pp164–65).

Include a pack of playing cards as it could prove a useful diversion if you find yourself in a survival predicament.

ENVIRONMENT-SPECIFIC GEAR
Mountains

In addition to the basic camping kit that has already been mentioned, anyone planning to travel in high, mountainous areas or snow-filled regions needs to be equipped with specialized kit to cope in a survival situation.

Group mountain kit

This kit will vary immensely according to the nature of the mountains but will generally include a good climbing rope and some slings, as well as specialized rock- or ice-climbing gear. Novices and inexperienced adventurers should not experiment in this terrain unless accompanied by an expert.

Above: *Ensure that your backpack is appropriate to your body size.*
Inset: *This climber is dressed for high-altitude climbing and sports many layers of clothing for warmth, and gaiters to prevent snow from sliding into the top of her boots.*

For mountainous areas and snow-filled regions, add the following equipment to your kit:

- **Ice axe** This is an essential tool for walking in ice-covered terrain with slopes that are more than very gently angled. A long walking axe is all that is needed for mountaineering not involving near-vertical slopes – terrain that is best left to specialist mountaineers. Fasten the axe securely to your belt or harness with a leash so that it cannot be lost if dropped.
- **Ski poles** When walking on snow and ice or traversing rough terrain, particularly on a downhill, ski poles are often more useful than a long ice axe. They help to prevent pressure on the knees.
- **Warm fleece clothing** This should be worn according to the principle of layering (see p46).
- **Lined parka jacket** A hooded rainproof parka will prevent loss of body heat.
- **Balaclava** This reduces the potentially considerable heat loss from the head.
- **Gloves** Many climbers wear several pairs of this important accessory – thin inner gloves, then thicker fleece or woollen mitts, covered by good-quality waterproof outer gloves.
- **Sturdy boots** These should be waterproof (Gore-Tex®-lined ones are a good choice) and able to accommodate your feet with at least two pairs of warm socks.
- **Gaiters** This handy cloth or nylon covering will help to keep snow out of the top of boots.
- **Overtrousers** Wind- and waterproof trousers or salopettes (quilted trousers held up by shoulder straps) are effective in keeping the legs dry and warm.
- **Sleeping bag** A very warm sleeping bag is a must. Down-filled types are warmer and lighter, but they compact into useless balls when wet. Synthetic fill is bulkier, but dries out relatively fast and retains its special insulating properties even after getting wet.
- **Foam insulating mat** A useful base to place under the sleeping bag.
- **Sunglasses** Essential eye protection against glaring UV light at altitude, they also prevent snow-blindness.

Caving adventures

Caving holds numerous dangers for the novice. Most people are unaccustomed to scrambling up or down in limited light and it is difficult to detect drop-offs or water with the interplay of light and shadow created by lamps. One should never attempt complex, difficult caves without considerable experience. No cave that requires ropework in the entrance, exit or any part of the route should be entered without trained guides and suitable equipment.

PERSONAL CAVING KIT

- **Clothing** If you envisage doing any crawling, wear sturdy trousers and a long-sleeved shirt. Tough boots or shoes are useful. As caves are seldom very cold, wearing thin, warmish clothing such as polypropylene undergarments beneath an overall are ideal.
- **Helmet** This is recommended to avoid bumping your head or sustaining injuries from small stones that may be dislodged by climbers above you. An alternative is to wear a woollen cap or felt hat for protection. Avoid hats with large rims as they prevent you from seeing what is happening above you.
- **Lamp** A head lamp is best to allow hands-free movement. Fasten it to the helmet with duct tape if it does not have a suitable strap. Do not stint on the quality and price of a lamp – reliable access to light in a dark cave environment is all-important.
- **Spare lamp** Each member of the group should ensure that they carry a good-quality spare lamp to cope with emergency situations.
- **Batteries and bulbs** Each person should carry at least one (preferably two) spare sets of batteries and a spare bulb. The latter can often be taped inside the lamp head or body.
- **Food and water** A small amount of food such as chocolate, energy bars and dried fruit is welcome and vital nourishment during a hard day's caving. Always remember to carry a full water bottle.
- **Pack** Take a small, tough pack in which to carry spare food and water.

A reliable light source is all-important when navigating through dark caves.

Rope: Use proper 'static' caving rope, which is made of material that is less susceptible to battery chemicals than normal climbing rope. This is useful to safeguard cavers on moderate, short slopes or tied around ankles to back-haul in tight passages. (Cave roping is a highly specialized pursuit and should only be attempted by those who are familiar with its technique.)

• **Strong string or nylon cord:** Useful to mark your way in complex underground passages. Ensure that the string is securely tied at the start and remove it when exiting the cave.

• **First-aid kit:** Take a kit to be able to cope with any minor abrasions and scratches, and other minor injuries.

Group caving kit

• **Spare lamp(s):** You have to have light in the dark interior of a cave. Many groups land in an unpleasant predicament when their only light source fails. Take at least one spare lamp, batteries and bulbs per group.

• **Candles and matches:** This is useful both for emergency light and to mark your return route. Take care to remove all traces of candlewax or matches and do not place lit candles where they can ruin sensitive dripstone formations.

• **Compass, paper and pencil:** These items are vital for keeping track of turns and directions taken while exploring caves. They can then be used for backtracking.

Head lamps and flashlights are vital when moving around in dark caves. Each member of the group should carry a reliable spare lamp.

Desert essentials

Travel in hot, arid areas needs specialized clothing and a suitable vehicle that is packed with certain basic essentials. It is important to be adequately prepared to deal with the desert extremes (hot temperatures during the day, and the drastic drop in temperatures during the night).

A hat provides some protection from the harsh rays of the desert sun.

Group desert kit

- **Extra water:** Any vehicle travelling through a desert area (even on good roads) should carry adequate emergency rations of water in case of a breakdown or accident. Carry the water in multiple containers rather than one large one to avoid losing your entire supply due to leakage or contamination with oil or other unpalatable substances.

A broad-spectrum sunscreen lotion should have an SPF of 20 or higher.

- **Plastic sail or groundsheet:** This can be used to create shade during the day and for extra warmth at night. Groundsheets can also be very useful to collect water through condensation or to make 'stills' from plants.

- **Vehicle spares:** Tyres, tools, and basic engine spares must be packed. Extra fuel, as well as a fanbelt, radiator hose, fuses and other vital parts (e.g. spark plugs, points and a condenser), should be carried for trips to remote wilderness areas which are often far away from 'civilization'.

- **Food:** Carry provisions that will last at least three days in the vehicle.

Water canteens, clockwise from top: a small bottle suitable for day hikes; bottle with sip tube; larger version for extended hiking; 'Camelback' container for longer adventure trips.

PERSONAL DESERT KIT

- **Clothing** This should be lightweight cotton, loose-fitting and light-coloured to reflect heat. Long-sleeved shirts and long trousers will prevent undue exposure to the sun.
- **T-shirt** This helps to keep the body cool by absorbing and dissipating perspiration from the skin.
- **Hat** A broad-brimmed with ventilation holes for the sun.
- **Sunglasses** A good-quality pair of sunglasses filters out UVA and UVB rays and prevents eye-strain in the harsh reflective glare of the desert.
- **Jacket** A warm, windproof jacket is needed as desert temperatures can drop drastically at night.
- **Sunscreen** A sunblock cream with a sun protection factor (SPF) of 20 or even higher helps to protect the skin from painful sunburn.

Shade can be created using a groundsheet. Rocks placed above your head should be stable in case of wind.

Jungles and tropical areas

These regions can be difficult to move through. The dense tangle of vegetation snares you and makes progress laboured, the atmosphere is uncomfortably humid and there is the prospect of encountering various insects and reptiles.

In these conditions, heat exhaustion poses as much of a threat as hypothermia does in cold areas – dehydration can be an unexpected hazard. Counter this by carrying plenty of liquid.

Waterproof shoes will keep your feet dry, while drawstring trousers prevent leeches from getting in.

- **Clothing:** This is essentially the same as for desert conditions, but tougher material is preferable.
- **Drawstring trousers:** These help to keep leeches and other crawling creatures out (elastic bands can also be used).
- **Mosquito-net fringe on hat:** This vital fringe can be fitted when needed, in the evening or when resting.
- **Machete or large knife:** This broad, heavy knife is very useful when cutting away vegetation.

Include a machete or a large knife in your kit, for cutting away vegetation.

- **Insect repellent:** This item is a must and should be applied to hands, arms and other exposed body parts. Avoid the forehead and around the eyes, as perspiration will sting the eyes.

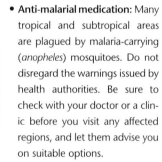

- **Anti-malarial medication:** Many tropical and subtropical areas are plagued by malaria-carrying (*anopheles*) mosquitoes. Do not disregard the warnings issued by health authorities. Be sure to check with your doctor or a clinic before you visit any affected regions, and let them advise you on suitable options.
- **Medical kit:** Injuries rapidly become infected in the tropics. Prevent any infections by covering wounds with a sterile, waterproof dressing and ensure that you have anti-fungal cream for your feet.
- **Mosquito net:** Suspended over your bed at night, this is a highly effective way to protect yourself against being bitten by mosquitoes.

Sea voyages

Ocean-going vessels are required by law to carry certain basic rescue and emergency gear, which includes life rafts (or life jackets on smaller craft), radio, flares, and often rescue beacons. Life rafts are indispensable when venturing into rough or potentially stormy waters. It is also valuable to have a comprehensive Survival Kit (see pp28–29) in an easily accessible pouch.

Check that any craft you are sailing in has the basic emergency stores and know where to find them.

A store-bought and an improvised gaff, with a small net. Any experienced fisherman will tell you that landing the fish you have hooked is half the battle.

- **Raft or dinghy:** These are usually easily inflatable and should be made of tough canvas or rubber. They must be stable, have plenty of places to hold on to and preferably have some form of built-in shelter. Ensure that there is basic survival gear (including water) on board.

- **Flares:** Both parachute flares and red hand-held or smoke flares greatly assist your chances of being seen by rescuers. (Expiry dates must be valid.)
- **Strobe lights:** Powerful, compact strobe lights are easily visible at night and can even be fastened onto individual life jackets.
- **Waterproof containers:** These are used to hold vital personal effects, as well as emergency rations, waterproof matches, maps and flares.
- **Sea anchor (drogue):** This can be streamed behind the boat to keep the bows facing into the direction of the weather and restrict drifting.
- **Gaff and net:** Invaluable for catching fish in extended survival conditions. Keep the gaff point embedded in cork or similar to avoid damaging the craft or injuring one of its occupants.
- **Cord:** Strong nylon cord has many uses in shipboard survival.

The wearing of a life jacket on sea craft is required by law.

Diving trips

A scuba diver will usually have an inflatable Buoyancy Compensator (BC) that has a whistle attached to it. This specialized 'life jacket' holds the scuba cylinder and can be inflated from it, or by mouth. It is used to control a diver's buoyancy and is usually fully inflated on the surface to keep the diver high in the water.

Some useful items to aid survival and rescue that can easily be stowed in the pouch of the BC include:

- **Signal buoy or surface-marker buoy:** This can be inflated by mouth or by using air from the diving cylinder. It projects far enough above the surface to make the diver visible to boats.

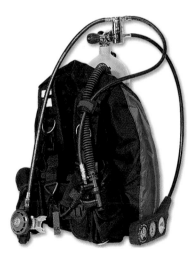

Buoyancy compensators (BC) are inflatable bladders and commonly jacket-styled.

This scuba diver is well prepared for any emergencies as she is carrying all the correct gear necessary for safe diving.

- **Strobe light:** Small, compact but very bright, this light is easily visible at night and even attracts attention in the daytime.
- **Waterproofed mini flares**: These can be seen from a long distance, particularly at night.

USING VEHICLES AND SPARE PARTS

In the event of a serious accident in which a vehicle is wrecked or rendered unusable, many parts can be used in the ensuing survival situation. Great care should be taken if there is still fuel in any tank(s), or if parts of the vehicle are likely to collapse and injure those inside. If there is any sign of spilt fuel, wait until the vehicle has cooled down completely. The first priority may be to make the vehicle interior suitable for shelter.

Many synthetic fabrics such as seat covers and cushions, as well as plastic mouldings, give off poisonous fumes as they burn or smoulder. Abandoning a vehicle may be a tough decision to have to make, and should only be considered if it outweighs the benefits of staying in or near it. Vehicles are usually more easily visible than people in air searches. If you do decide to move away from the vehicle, consider what can be removed and taken along to your advantage.

Many vehicle parts can be used (below). This air filter (above) can make a useful cup or scoop after rinsing it clean.

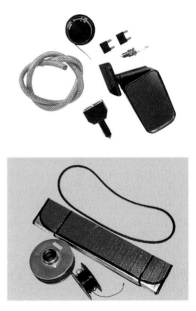

A stiff floor mat can be rolled into an effective splint, or used to handle warm objects, or for additional insulation in cold regions.

A sun shield can act as reflector for fires, and as a 'space blanket'; fan belts make tough slings; air filters pre-filter water; electrical wire is used as a cord.

USEFUL VEHICLE PARTS

- **Hubcaps** make good pots and water carriers.
- **Mirrors** can be used for signalling.
- **Tyres** cut into pieces can make tough hardy sandal soles and can also be used effectively for fuel and for signal smoke.
- **Inner tubes** are useful water carriers although the water may subsequently not taste too good. They can also be used as flotation devices across rivers, fuel, slingshot bands, elastic bandages and for carrying loads.
- **Radiators** have a good water supply, however: DO NOT DRINK WATER FROM ANY RADIATOR THAT MAY HAVE CONTAINED ANTIFREEZE, EVEN AFTER DISTILLATION. Radiator fluid can also be used for cooling stills or cleaning items.
- **Grease or oil** can be used to light fires and can also be smeared on as a deterrent against mosquitoes and other insects.
- **Battery and light** can be used for night-time signals. The battery is also useful to start fires, or to power radios, cellphones (mobile phones), etc. Be sure not to overload the battery's voltage limit.
- **Tools (e.g. screwdrivers)** can make very handy weapons, as well as digging and hunting tools.
- **Roofracks/ladders/bonnets/cargo mats** can be used as sledges and to transport goods or injured group members.
- **Air filters** make a good stove base if they are one of the metal-framed models, while some can even be used as a pre-filter in purifying water.
- **Seat covers** can be used as additional cover, for straining liquids, and as bandages and supports in first-aid situations.
- **Window glass** is a very useful signalling device, the larger the better, to attract attention.
- **Seats and carpets** can be used to create shelter 'tunnels', or for insulation as a groundsheet.
- **Electrical flex** is effective as a fishing line, for starting fires and for tying or fastening objects.
- **Maps and charts** may give some indication where you are and which way to go if movement is your best option.

BASIC TOOLS

Tools in survival situations generally take the place of knives, hammers or saws. In some cases, basic tools may even become hunting implements or be used as weapons.

If planning carefully, you will take some store-bought items along with you on your outing.

An all-purpose, fold-up knife is very handy in the wild.

- **Penknife:** A sharp, strong penknife (folding-blade knife) is a valuable tool. Keep it attached to your belt or your body with a lanyard. The authentic Swiss Army knives are tough and versatile as they have many useful blades, including screwdrivers, saws, and awls (a pointed tool with a fluted blade for piercing wood). Some versions even have built-in scissors and tweezers.

- **Sheath knife:** A strong sheath knife (fixed-blade knife) is indispensable in the wild; choose one that has a solid tang going right through the handle as this can be used even if the wooden or plastic handle breaks. It is always a good idea to have a sheath that holds the knife securely and has a loop for a belt.

- **Survival knife:** Some experts prefer a hollow-handled style of knife, which can carry some survival kit and easily be turned into a spear. If you do choose one of these, make sure it is a strong one. Any large, sharp knife with a serrated piece for a sawblade is also suitable. A robust sheath with an

effective clip protects the knife and prevents it being lost.

- **Kukri, parang or machete:** These are all large, heavy, powerful hybrids between a knife and an axe, used for hunting, cutting wood and clearing away vegetation. The kukri is the traditional tool of the Nepalese, while the parang is used in Malaysia. Machetes are used worldwide in bush or jungle areas and are extremely useful. The weight and size of the machete blade makes it as effective as an axe for felling small trees.

- **Axe:** If you are lucky enough to have an axe, treat it with care – it is one of the most valuable tools in the bush.

- **Multi-purpose tools:** Multi-blade tools such as Leatherman® fulfil a host of functions as they feature solid blades, useful pliers and saws. These multi-purpose devices are well worth the investment and no serious adventure traveller should be without one.

MAKING UTENSILS

Useful tools can be created from diverse sources including glass, metal or the tough plastic parts of vehicles. Before leaving a vehicle, make sure that you have stripped it of all useful parts.

Creating tools

This guideline indicates the type of tools you can make if you find yourself in a survival situation.

- **Stone tools** Prehistoric man made efficient tools from bone, stone and other natural objects. This is not as easy as it sounds but can be done with persistence and practice. To create stone tools, split flakes off a large, solid piece of rock with softer stones (for smaller, finer flakes use hard pieces of wood or bone). Heavy smooth black rock such as flint or obsidian makes good tools. Stone tools can be used as scrapers, knives, spear points, arrowheads, as well as axeheads.

- **Wooden tools** A simple but effective tool or weapon is a wooden spear – whittle the end of a 2m (6ft) hard-wood pole, then temper (harden) the point with a few seconds of repeated heating and cooling in a fire. Continually rotate the point while you do this.

- **Glass knife** A shard of glass wrapped in leather or cloth can be a very effective tool, particularly for gutting fish or other animals. To make one from a bottle, wrap the bottle thoroughly in cloth, then tap it firmly on a hard surface. Open the cloth, watching for sharp shards of glass. Select a long piece with a sharp edge and thick base for a handle. A robust covering on the handle section is essential to prevent injury to the user. Tie this on with tape, string or use any other suitable alternative.

- **Bamboo knife** Bamboo can be made into an effective tool or hunting spear for smaller animals or a shovel for dig-  ging out roots and bulbs. Cut a long section of bamboo at one end at an angle to create a point. If you have no knife, break bamboo by snapping it over a tree branch until you get a suitable sharp end. Sharpen it further by rubbing it on a rough surface.

- **Slingshot** Much easier to make than a catapult, but this David-and-Goliath weapon is far more difficult to use. All you need is a piece of leather (or tough cloth) for the pouch and two lengths of rope or twine for the thongs. Make a hole in each side of the pouch and attach the thongs. Smooth stones work best in this slingshot. The key to using a slingshot effectively is to work up a good speed when twirling it above your head, then release one thong in the correct direction. Make sure you have no-one near you when trying out your slingshot, as your direction will be unpredictable for a good number of attempts. Slingshots are capable of killing large animals.

- **Catapults** A catapult is most useful in catching small game such as birds, rodents and even small buck. Use hard, solid wood or tough greenish wood to make the V-shaped handle; an inner tube makes  superb elastic, and a piece of leather (your wallet, or the tongue of your shoe) the pouch. River pebbles are generally the best ammunition; another option is to use ball bearings from your vehicle.

- **Throwing stick** The simplest of all weapons can be a throwing stick or simply a stone, which can be surprisingly efficient. In extreme survival situations that call for killing game and birds, these might produce good results. Choose or cut a solid, moderately heavy stick about .5m (1½ft) long, prefer- ably one with a small knob (e.g. a truncated branch) on the end. Smooth down the handle to ensure an easy release. When using the throwing stick, spin it by flicking your wrist at the end of the throwing stroke, as it will have more chance of hitting the game.

CLOTHING AND SHELTER

With the exception of air and sea disasters, you should have decided what clothing you will need for your trip well in advance. By selecting clothing to accommodate 'worst case scenarios', you will ensure that you can cope and improvise if the group is thrust into an unexpected climatic situation by a disaster.

Cold conditions – either at sea or on land – pose by far the greatest danger. However, extremes of heat and humidity can also create problems to those without appropriate shelter or clothing. In a survival situation, building shelter is all about improvisation.

Hiking in warm conditions, people usually prefer wearing thin clothing; this is fine but always take along extra warm clothing in case there is a drop in the temperature.

CLOTHING FOR COLD CLIMATES

Cold is a killer, and wet and windy conditions can often intensify the effects of low temperatures. Always take enough clothing to cope with unpredictable weather changes, particularly at sea and in high mountain areas.

In cold climates, follow the principles of layering. Multiple clothing layers trap warm air, providing effective insulation against the cold.

- **Inner layer** – a warm, absorbent layer of polypropylene or a similar 'wicking' fabric (these fabrics absorb moisture away from the skin) next to the body.
- **Middle layer(s)** – usually a thick cotton, nylon, or preferably fleece shirt and a good-quality down garment, which is very light relative to its insulating value. Alternative options are wool, polar fleece or any other similar thick-pile fibres.

- **Outer layer** – should be wind- and waterproof; the best material is a breathable fabric, such as Gore-Tex®, which reduces the build-up of perspiration around your body.
- **Extremities** – two pairs of socks (one thin and one thick pair), gloves and a balaclava. Up to 25 per cent of body heat can be lost via an uncovered head and neck area, and a further 20 per cent through the hands and feet.

Choices of material

When deciding on the most suitable material, remember that down loses its insulating value when wet, and is difficult to dry out, whereas fleece material retains a good deal of insulation and dries easily. If you are heading for an area which you know will be cold and dry, then down is the best option; if it is cold and wet, your best choice would be garments made from thick fleece.

In the event of an accident or unexpected poor weather, you may not even get close to this ideal and you may need to rely heavily on improvisation. Remember that even in temperate areas, persons in shock should always be kept warm.

In all areas, being thoroughly prepared for all the likely weather conditions greatly increases your chances of surviving in comfort.

In cold conditions, wear a balaclava and gloves, according to the principles of layering, to prevent further heat loss.

TIPS ON IMPROVISED EMERGENCY CLOTHING

- **Parachutes, sails and even tents** (if you have spare or do not need them) can be cut into pieces to make an easy covering. Try to cut large pieces so that these can later be sewn into more user-friendly clothes if the need arises.
- **Carpets** provide a reasonable amount of insulation and warmth, especially for sitting or lying on.
- **Seat covers** with holes cut in the sides make effective jackets, and can also be used for socks or leggings.
- **Thin foam mattresses** are useful for body wrapping. If on the move, they can be used as a type of jacket.
- **Vegetation** such as large leaves makes a very handy covering if nothing else is available.
- **Tents** can be used to make temporary shelters and provide warmth when wrapped around someone in shock or suffering from hypothermia. A tent can also be rolled up and used as a covering in windy conditions or in the dark.

SHELTER

The need to shelter from the elements often goes hand in hand with wearing appropriate clothing. Wind, sun and cold all affect the body and you will need to escape or find protection from some or all of these conditions. If you are in a desperate situation and are fortunate, you may have a good tent available, or you may find natural shelters such as caves, overhangs or hollows nearby. If neither is available you will have to create or improvise a temporary shelter. The psychological bonus of having any form of 'home' should also not be underestimated – a great deal of personal security is linked to having a roof over one's head. As survival focuses so much on one's state of mind, shelter should always be seen as more than merely a physical necessity.

Man-made shelters
Tents

If you have a tent with you, it is possible to camp under quite extreme conditions. By building windbreaks out of rocks, logs or banks of earth or snow and using these to help anchor the tent, you can withstand high winds. Even heavy rain and snow should not be a real problem provided that you dig channels next to the tent to drain the site and clear off the snow before it breaks poles.

Some tents are made of a single breathable material like Gore-Tex®. This material is usually only used in light-weight, high-altitude, extreme mountaineering tents and is very expensive. Most other quality tents usually have an inner, breathable nylon layer, with a waterproof outer section suspended a small distance above it to allow air to circulate freely and facilitate the removal of body-generated condensation. Ensure that your tent has a built-in groundsheet of a good quality to prevent any water seeping up from the ground.

There are three basic types of tents – geodesic, A-frame and tunnel.

Inuit placing the top keystone in an igloo.

- **Geodesic** is extremely wind-resistant, and thus suited for use in mountains with high winds and snowfall; has the highest strength-to-weight ratio. Those tents with three or preferably four poles are more stable than those with only two.

- **A-frame**, also known as a ridge tent; has plenty of headroom and is often less expensive than a geodesic tent. However, it is not as stable in windy conditions.

- **Tunnel** is fairly stable and lighter for its size than geodesic types. These tents are not as good in heavy snow but are a good choice in wind.

Ideally, you should pitch your tent away from a steep slope, but not in a basin where you may encounter flooding. If there is a river in the vicinity, check the river flow and be sure not to camp below any possible flood levels. Take note of wind patterns and try to shelter the tent by placing it in the lee of bushes, rocks or trees. When camping in snow, be alert to the possibilities of avalanches and site your tent well away from any potential avalanche zone.

If you do happen to get caught out in the open without any form of tent or access to a man-made shelter, the easiest and fastest option is to seek out a natural feature that can be used as makeshift shelter.

- **Cave or deep overhang** This is a boon if you can find one. Always check for tracks at the entrance to ensure that the cave is not inhabited by an animal. Cover the entrance with brush, branches or other material to maintain warmth and shield you from the elements.
- **Hollows** A hollow or a space under a rock can provide welcome shelter from the wind. Roof it with small branches and any other suitable material you can find in the surrounding area.
- **Logs and fallen trees** A temporary lean-to shelter can be formed relatively easily by scraping out a small depression on the lee side of a log and placing branches or twigs over it.
- **Under snow-laden trees** Natural depressions form in the snow under the branches of conifers found in forests in the Northern Hemisphere. This space can be enlarged by digging down into snow drifts.

Constructed shelters
Cold conditions

Shelter from the wind is often a high priority in cold conditions. Inside a snow shelter, the temperature can remain at a comfortable zero instead of a temperature potentially far lower in the open. Lifesaving options include a trench dug in the snow and roofed by a groundsheet or branches packed with snow, and a snow cave dug in a bank or glacier. If you need to stay outdoors for

Dig a hollow into the snow to make an ice-cave shelter.

longer, construct a good snow shelter. A trench in the snow can be roofed with blocks of snow and reinforced with branches or other available material. This is a useful short-term shelter for one or two people.

BUILDING A QUINZE

A quinze is a simple form of igloo built from compacted snow.

- Stack backpacks or suitable equipment to form a pyramidal heap about 1m (3ft) high.
- Pack snow onto and around this pile of gear. Each 5–10cm (2–4in) layer must be very well compacted by hand, and left to 'freeze' for about 20 minutes.
- When the structure has formed a dome about 1.5m (4ft) high and 2.5–3m (7–10ft) in diameter, push short sticks if available (if not, improvise) into a depth of about 25cm (10in). This will help you to judge the thickness of the snow when hollowing the quinze out.

- Dig an entrance and then take out the core of the snow until the packs or gear can be removed. Hollow the quinze out until you touch the bottom of the sticks. Use your hands to compact the snow on the inside.
- Once inside the structure, use a pack or other suitable item to partially close the entrance and help preserve warmth.

SIMPLE SHELTERS

In tropical environments, most aspects of shelter construction will rely on improvisation, depending on the circumstances and what materials are available. The useful ideas given here may need to be modified to accommodate a particular situation.

- **Constructing a tepee** Lash a few poles of similar length together at one end (the top). Push the rough structure up into the air and spread the poles evenly apart. Digging small holes into the ground to accommodate the pole bases will make the structure more stable.

  Cover the poles with canvas or other suitable material; use small branches if nothing else is available.
- **A-frame construction** You can create an effective waterproof A-frame construction by using a canvas sheet, grass or small branches and leaves. In warm regions, bamboo makes excellent building material, but be careful as it can create dangerously sharp splinters when it is cut or split.

Tepee

A-Frame

Sleeping platforms

Damp ground and crawling insects are part of temperate and tropical forest, and it is always wise to elevate your sleeping platform above the ground. Even for sleeping under the stars, a sleeping platform is a good idea. If you are creating some form of shelter, try to incorporate a raised sleeping platform into the design.

After you have constructed the roof of your rough tepee or A-frame, make a sleeping platform inside the structure. Form a frame with four to six upright poles or branches, then lash horizontal support poles across the ends and sides of the frame. Add numerous crosspieces a few spaces apart on which to place your makeshift mattress of leaves and branches or any other suitable material. It is much easier to incorporate a sleeping platform into an A-frame construction. Simply lash horizontal support poles directly to the frame on at least one side of the shelter and layer with bedding material.

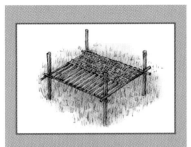

Sleeping platform shows cross-piece construction

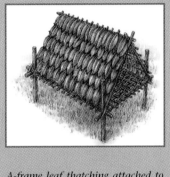

A-frame leaf thatching attached to sleeping platform

Temperate/grassland shelters

Temporary shelters in temperate or grassland areas are essentially similar to those you would construct in a jungle or tropical area. However, providing shade and perhaps protection from marauding animals would be more important than focusing on a rain- or windproof shelter.

It may be necessary to thatch grass over twigs if you need to make the structure sun- or waterproof. This is a time-consuming process but less elaborate if you simply have to create shade. As with jungle shelters, raise the sleeping platform off the ground if you have enough time and suitable materials available.

FINDING SHELTER IN THE DESERT

In desert environments, the temperature extremes demand shelter from daytime heat and nights that are frequently cold. These both result from the dry air and lack of insulation. Air does not retain heat without a reasonable moisture content; therefore the sun's rays are scorching during the day, but the dry air allows the daytime heat to rapidly dissipate at night.

- **During the day** Use a sail, groundsheet, piece of cloth or any other available material such as a sleeping bag. Preferably, lift the shelter off the ground by piling up sticks, stones or your backpack as a base to benefit from the circulating air flow.
- **At night** The same materials can be used to improve insulation. Many desert nomads dig a hole in the sand, and then lay their robes in the hollow. By wrapping in a sail and piling as much sand as possible on top of themselves, they create effective protection against the bitterly cold desert nights.

An ideal, natural desert shelter affords good shade and allows any breeze to blow through.

Use rocks to weight down sheeting over a natural depression for protection in a mild sandstorm.

If you have no form of cover during the daytime, try to locate even the smallest amount of shade cast by rock outcrops or desert plants, however sparse. Covering yourself with desert plants, no matter how dry and scanty they are, will help to some extent. Digging into the sand will cause you to heat up, but if you dig fairly deep, you should be able to reach cooler sand. Climb into the hole and cover yourself with a layer of sand to help shield your exposed skin from harmful ultraviolet (UV) rays.

Vicious sandstorms are common occurrences in the desert. If you get caught in one, try to find shelter, sit with your back to the wind and cover your entire body. By wrapping a cloth loosely around your head, you will still be able to breathe while shielding yourself from the stinging sand that is blowing all around you.

A scarf, shawl or piece of cloth wrapped around the face in a sandstorm allows you to breathe but filters out the sand.

In a severe storm, seek any available shelter, crouch low and protect your face and body.

KNOTS AND LASHINGS

Many temporary shelters as well as bridges, flotation devices and other items entail tying poles together. This implies knowledge of knots and some form of rope. It is easy to learn basic rope-tying techniques with some practice; however, rope may not be readily available and you will probably have to devise your own.

HOW TO PREVENT ROPE ENDS FROM UNRAVELLING

Sealing nylon ropes: To prevent the nylon from unravelling, burn the rope ends. These can also be sealed by pressing or rolling the ends with a very hot piece of metal.

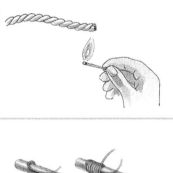

Whipping: This method is used to prevent the ends of multi-core ropes from unravelling, and on sisal and fibre ropes which cannot be heat-fused. Whipping, where thin cord is wrapped around the thicker rope, creates added grip to axe handles, knives or the handles of stretchers which need to be carried over distance.

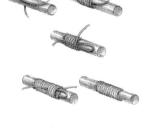

BASIC USEFUL KNOTS

Practise knots and lashings until you can do them easily and swiftly.

Reef knot with half-hitches: One of the most common knots; it is used to tie ropes of similar thickness together. Ties fairly easily. Safer when finished with a half-hitch or two on either side.

Sheet bend; double sheet bend: Ties two rope ends of differing thicknesses together. Unties easily. Double sheet bend is safer, but more complicated to do.

Overhand loop: A quick and easy knot that holds well under load, it can be tied at the end or middle of a rope. Useful for making nets or joining rope ends.

Figure of eight: This knot is tied quickly and is less likely to slip. Climbers use this knot to attach a rope to a carabiner fixed on a climbing harness.

BASIC USEFUL KNOTS

Rewoven figure of eight: Used to make a loop around an anchor point; also, to tie rope directly onto a climber's harness. The two ends lie constantly parallel and emerge at the same end.

Round turn and two half-hitches: Secures a line to a post. Easily tied, even when the rope is under tension.

Clove hitch: Good for starting or ending lashings; both ends can take strain. Can be used in the middle of a rope if the rope is slipped around the end of a spar or beam.

Timber hitch: Used in lashings or to attach a beam or log that is being dragged. An extra half-hitch can be added to hold heavy spars.

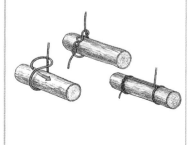

LASHINGS

Square lashing: Used wherever poles cross at right angles, e.g. rafts and stretchers.

- Start with a clove hitch or timber hitch under the crosspiece.
- Take the rope several times over and under the crosspiece, pulling tightly.
- Make a full turn around the horizontal pole so you can wrap in the opposite direction for four turns. Secure with a few half-hitches or a clove hitch.

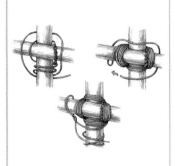

Shear (diagonal) lashing: Joins poles that meet on the diagonal, or any angle other than a right angle. Used in tepees, A-frame bridges or shelters.

- Tie a clove hitch on one spar, then do a few loose horizontal turns around both spars. Loop several vertical frapping (tightening) turns between spars.
- You then finish with a clove hitch on the second spar.

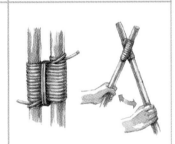

Improvised cord and rope: Vehicles have material in the form of electric wire, cord in carpets, seat covers, or nylon bands in some tyres; vines, grass, the bark of some trees, leaves and animal hair make cord.

- Plait several lengths (plait tightly when working with natural fibres), then plait three pieces together in order to make a much stronger rope.

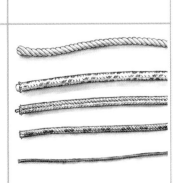

FOOD AND WATER

When faced with an unexpected survival situation, food and water immediately become a priority. Since water is far more important to the body than food, it is wise to immediately find a suitable supply of water and then set out to find food. Bear in mind that most water on earth is contaminated and will need to be filtered and purified. If a portable commercial water filter is not available, you will need to construct makeshift filters and stills to purify water from the environment.

Although we are conditioned to regard food as a daily necessity, it is possible to go without food for several weeks. This chapter teaches you methods of obtaining and purifying water, testing plants and finding other sources of food that are safe for human consumption.

When faced with a survival situation, focus on your number one priorities – water, food, clothing and shelter. Immediately ration your food and water supply.

61

WATER
Locating water

Water is far more important than food in order to survive. The body can go for weeks without food, but for only a few days without water before it begins to deteriorate rapidly and severely.

Under normal conditions, a moderately active person needs 2–4 litres (4–8pt) of water per day. In true survival conditions you would need more, but you will probably have less than this available. If you find yourself in a situation where it appears that you may run out of water, never assume that rescue will get to you in time. Take an inventory of all water and other liquid supplies you have available and enforce a strict regime to conserve and ration them.

The presence of vegetation in the valley indicates a possible source of deep, underground water.

CONSERVING BODY FLUIDS

- To maintain your body's fluid balance, ensure that the water intake equals that which is excreted.
- Try to avoid eating dry, salty foods.
- Even in very cold conditions, a good deal of water is lost while you are breathing because of the dryness of the air. Breathe through the nose and not the mouth.
- Restrict your activity to an essential minimum to help preserve your body's water content.
- A negative water balance (staying slightly 'thirsty') right from the start will diminish your urine output and aid water retention later, when your body needs it most.

SOURCES OF WATER FROM THE ENVIRONMENT

• **Rainwater:** almost universally safe, except after a large volcanic eruption or huge fire. When it rains, try to collect rainwater and store as much as you can in suitable containers.

Dig for underground water in dry riverbeds.

• **Ice and snow:** Ice is easier and quicker to melt than snow. If forced to use snow, then dig down beneath the surface, as deeper layers lower down are more granular and provide denser snow.

Sea ice has a lot of salt in it, except for older weathered ice (such as icebergs), recognizable by its bluish tinge. Survivors have found that the best way to obtain water from snow if there is no fuel to melt it, is to form it into compact balls. These should either be exposed to the sun or placed next to one's body in some form of waterproof container. Place the ice balls in black plastic bags if you have them. Remove the ice balls from the plastic and suck water from the bottom of them.

LOCATING WATER IN DRY CONDITIONS

• Remember that water always runs to the lowest possible point.
• When searching for water, start by trying to reach higher ground or climb a tree to scan the terrain for riverbeds. Water can often be found in seemingly dry riverbeds if one digs deep enough.
• The best areas to start digging for water are those where there is some sign of green vegetation and where the riverbed or stream takes a sharp turn on the outside bank or meets a rock barrier.
• In mountainous areas, search at the base of cliffs or in sheltered crevices.
• On beaches, dig down above the high-water mark and once you hit damp sand, allow time for the water to trickle in. It may be brackish but it is drinkable, particularly once it has been distilled though the sand.

Jungle and tropics

Most jungles and tropical areas will have rainfall, often on a daily basis. Remember to have containers available to collect any rainfall. Large-leafed plants are a good source of run-off water – tie a few leaves together so that their tips angle downwards into your container.

Vines make an excellent water source but avoid those that excrete a milky sap, as this is usually poisonous.

- Palm and banana trees have a good supply of water in their trunks. Cut a banana tree off close to the ground and make a hollow bowl in the stump with a sharp object. The hollow will fill with water and although it may take a few hours, it provides clean water that is safe to drink.
- To obtain water from bamboo stems, cut a notch at the bottom of a section and let the water drain out. Older bamboo often holds more free water than young, green bamboo. Some vines have drinkable water in them – but avoid those with a milky sap, as this is usually poisonous. Note also that certain vines may produce an allergic skin reaction, although their water is perfectly safe to drink.
- To obtain water from a vine, cut a notch as high as possible to release the water, then cut the vine low down to allow the water to drain out. Vines with drinkable water produce copious amounts of free-flowing liquid and are round, not flat. Water from suitable vines will have a slightly fruity or neutral taste and will seem palatable to drink.

Many larger-leafed jungle plants have water trapped in the area where the leaves meet the stem, including some of the large and attractive orchids, as well as bromeliads and pitcher plants. Palm tree stems can contain water that is most easily accessed by cutting the tip off a flowering stalk and bending it downwards. Coconut milk is safe, but ripe fruits have a strong laxative effect.

Observing wild animals and birds

- Follow animal tracks or the flight pattern of birds. Most animals and birds drink in the early morning hours or late in the afternoon.
- Bear in mind that animal tracks can be misleading. As a general rule: if they lead downhill and converge, they could lead to water.

Studying animal patterns may lead you to water sources.

- Birds flying towards water usually approach fast and in a straight line, and in a more meandering pattern away from it. Ducks and geese fly to water in the early morning hours and away at night. Doves and pigeons usually fly to water in small groups, but return in flocks.
- Larger fish often have a small amount of accessible water alongside their vertebral column. The fluid can be obtained by carefully gutting the fish and removing the backbone.

GETTING WATER FROM PLANTS

- Cacti and aloe species are excellent water sources.
- Plant roots often contain stores of water, especially in dry areas. Dig down and cut the root. Then crush it and extract its water by squeezing the pulp through a piece of cloth.
- Dew that condenses on plants, particularly those with broad leaves, can be a valuable water source. You could also try a method used by the Australian Aborigines, who collect moisture from dew by tying bunches of grass to their ankles and then walking through the grass fields.

Prickly pear fruit is tasty and contains much water. They must be peeled before they can be eaten.

WATER PURIFICATION AND FILTRATION

Most of the world's water has been contaminated by the activities of man – either by heavy metals and other toxins or by human faeces. Some of these substances are impossible to remove by virtually any means. Although they might constitute a long-term health hazard, such traces are not of major importance in survival situations.

Human (and in some cases, animal) faeces are a different matter – these harbour microorganisms such as Giardia as well as other bacteria and viruses that can swiftly lead to health problems. The concept of a 'pristine mountain stream' is almost a modern myth, as even some of the world's most isolated streams carry considerable debris resulting from careless human toilet habits along their flow.

Despite claims to the contrary, most available portable water filters do not

Staying close to a river or stream is sometimes the best option, especially if you are uncertain of the area. You might not find another water supply for days.

remove all bacteria and microorganisms, in particular viruses, let alone chemicals.

Filtered water should be further sterilized by using purification tablets to make it completely safe. If you go from sea level to 4000m (12,500ft) or above, it is wise to treat the water with either chlorine or iodine water purification tablets. Another effective purification alternative is to add five drops of household bleach to a litre of water, then allow it to stand for 45 minutes. The water does tend to have a strange taste, but you can rest assured that it is biologically safe to drink.

Commercial water filter

Items that can be used to carry or store water after cleansing (clockwise from top): part of an air filter scoop; a hat lined with a plastic bag; a gourd made from a desert melon; a plastic liner in a box.

Transporting water

Transporting water to your camp site or on the move can be a problem. Plastic bags, silvered wine bags or waterproof containers can be invaluable. Gourds can also be made out of some plants such as melons, bamboo and squashes.

Filtering water

Much of the water you will find will be murky, containing sediment and small pieces of plant and animal matter.

- First, filter out all particles by using a good commercial filter or you can devise your own filter from coffee filter papers, car air filters, handkerchiefs or even old socks.
- If all you find is mud, place it in a piece of cloth, and wring the moisture out into a container.

- With any water-containing vegetation, crush the plant in a cloth to extract the liquid.
- If you dig a water hole in the sand, prevent it from collapsing on itself by lining it with plant material.
- If all makeshift methods fail and there is no water supply, filter as much as you can using stone and sand filters, and then drink the water – any diseases can in all likelihood be cured after you have been rescued.

Water that is locked into mud or vegetation can be squeezed out and strained in this way. The resulting liquid still needs to be purified.

Clean sea water can be used to cook food.

Stills to purify water

A good, efficient still can be used to make sea water and other fluids (e.g. radiator fluid and suspect water collected from different sources) safe to drink. Unless the still is 100 per cent efficient (highly unlikely in field conditions) the water is unlikely to be 'pure', and may still have a strange taste and/or harbour microorganisms.

A method to condense and purify sea water.

This method collects water from plant transpiration.

- Place a container in a larger container or at the base of a hole roughly 40cm (15in) deep and 50cm (20in) across.
- Add vegetation to the larger container to produce water through transpiration.
- Cover the large hole with a piece of plastic.
- Weight the centre of the plastic with a stone so it dips towards the small container in the middle.
- Alternatively, to condense and purify seawater, a small container can be placed in a larger one holding the seawater, to act as a receptacle for the distilled fluid (see below left).

ACTIVE (STEAM) STILL

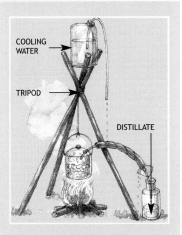

COOLING WATER

TRIPOD

DISTILLATE

In the event of a vehicle wreck or breakdown, you might well have the materials to produce a workable steam still. Any cracks or joints in the distillation tube can be sealed using mud or clay.

• A semi-sealed container contains liquid to be distilled and is suspended from a sturdy tripod over the fire.
• A distillation tube runs from the container to distillate bottle.
• Cooling (sea) water speeds up condensation by dripping onto a jacket wrapped around the distillation tube to distil the liquid more efficiently.

PLANT STILL

Most trees and plants transpirate ('sweat') a lot of water daily as part of their natural water and food transport system.

• You need a small bush or you can gather a pile of freshly cut vegetation to create a 'bag still'.
• Select a large plastic bag, if possible, and tie it tightly around the small bush, or around a branch with a good supply of leaves.
• If you use cut vegetation, place twigs so that they keep the bag from collapsing; for the small bush, surround it with the bag, ensuring that all openings are properly sealed.
• Water will collect in the low-lying corners of the bag.

OBTAINING FOOD

Although you need a fair amount of food when exercising, your body is capable of going without food for long periods of time. In a survival situation food should, nonetheless, be rationed very carefully. Remember that any plant a monkey (NOT a baboon) eats is usually edible to man. This is not true for other animals and birds – many consume plants or seeds that can be harmful to humans.

Sea lettuce is nutritious and quite easy to harvest.

LOCATING FOOD FROM PLANTS

- **Palm trees** The coconuts and other fruits as well as the soft heart of the young stem or branches can all be eaten.
- **Pine trees** When dug out of the cones, the seeds of this tree form a tasty, nutty food source. The leaves can be boiled to provide a type of tea.
- **Lichens** This safe, non-poisonous food needs to be boiled to soften it. Lichens can also be used to create a watery soup.
- **Sea lettuce** Marine algae are usually edible. Although there is no truly poisonous seaweed, some can cause stomach irritation, however. The common sea lettuce and kelp are found along beaches around the world, and both make safe and nutritious meals. They should first be washed, then boiled. Do not discard the leftover water, it makes a nutritious soup.
- **Nuts and nut-like seeds** These are found on many plants and are an excellent source of much-needed protein. Fortunately, very few nuts are poisonous or harmful.
- **Fern species** Many types of ferns, particularly those found in the Northern Hemisphere, can be eaten. None are poisonous except for mature plants of the bracken fern (*Pteridium aquilinum*), which is the most common species. To be safe, it is better to eat only young ferns – those with tightly coiled fronds. Remove the irritating little hairs that cover many fern species.

TESTING PLANTS

- Only one person should test each plant type.
- Test leaves, stems, seeds or fruits, and roots or tubers individually.
- Smell: if a plant smells of almonds (hydrocyanic acid) or peaches (prussic acid) when crushed, discard it immediately.
- Skin: rub a piece of crushed plant lightly on a soft skin area (e.g. inside of the arm). Wait at least five minutes; check if any rash, swelling or burning appears.
- Mouth and surrounds: place a small portion on the lips, then the corner of the mouth and the tip of the tongue. Chew a small amount, but don't swallow. Wait at least 10 seconds between each phase. Watch for any numbness, stinging sensation, soreness or burning.
- Swallowing: chew and swallow a small amount, then wait for at least three to four hours before eating anything else.

Perform the same tests for cooked plants, especially the swallowing test. Cooking may alter the chemical substances.

DO NOT EAT PLANTS UNTIL YOU HAVE TESTED THEM THOROUGHLY AND ARE SURE THEY ARE SAFE.

Nuts are one of the safest sources of food in the wild.

You can determine whether a plant is poisonous by smelling it.

Animals as a food source

Mankind can survive quite happily on a completely vegetarian diet, and it is often the easiest food to obtain.

You may need to make the decision to turn to animals. Smaller animals (including insects, grubs, marine invertebrates, molluscs and reptiles, fish and birds) can be easier to accept as a food source and are often simpler to trap or catch than the larger animals. Grubs, which tunnel inside dead or decaying trees, taste like roasted peanuts when fried. Make a point of avoiding very brightly coloured insects, as some are poisonous.

Above: *To make invertebrates more palatable, it is advisable to remove their wings, legs and hard outer casing.*

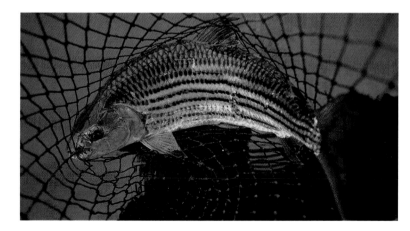

In some fish species, mucus on the skin may be toxic; if it feels slimy, wash it thoroughly or rub with sand before cooking.

Animal patterns

Animals, like humans, are creatures of habit. They follow set patterns of feeding and drinking and many make permanent burrows or homes. The first thing to do in a survival situation when food is becoming a priority is to look for traces left by animals and birds.

It is often easier to accept smaller animals as a food source. Reptiles make a nourishing snack, and it is less difficult to catch than larger animals.

- Examine paths through the bush – however faint – to establish whether animals regularly move along them.
- Study the tracks; you may obtain valuable information on the size, numbers and even the type of animal that uses them.
- It would be far easier to catch an

Trapping a bird in its nest can be tricky, as it is at its most cautious here.

animal on its regular route, or trap it in its nest or burrow, than to stalk it in the open.
- Hibernating animals in colder areas are easier to remove or dig out once you have found their lair.

It is pointless trying to trap the larger carnivores – their meat is usually rank and difficult to eat and it can easily make you sick. Herbivores such as buck, as well as some smaller carnivores and omnivores (e.g. seals, birds and monkeys), are usually far more suitable prey.

Small reptiles and amphibians – with the exception of warty toads – are all edible. However, remove the skin (some have glands in the skin that secrete a harmful mucus). Lizards, geckoes and snakes are excellent potential food sources. In the case of snakes, cut the head off well behind the mouth to avoid contact with any poison glands.

TRAPS AND SNARES

The aim of this chapter is not to encourage people in non-survival situations to head for the wild, build traps and snares, and catch animals. Prior knowledge of how to construct these traps, however, would be very helpful in a real survival situation. If you do practise your skill and accidentally catch an animal, treat it with dignity. Try to avoid injury, and release it if you can. Dismantle any snare or trap before you leave the area.

Snares and traps can be made with various materials and devising your own version is a key element.

Fish are wary creatures so avoid casting a shadow on the surface of the water; also, they tend to concentrate in a calm, deep, shaded pool of water when the temperature is warm, and along the edges of sunny patches when it is cool.

SNARES AND TRAPS

Wire, flex, cord or string – if you have them at hand – are invaluable if you wish to construct an effective trap and can also be used to build many different types. If you do not have any of the above available, you will probably need to improvise and construct deadfall traps, pits, or balance traps. Trapping and hunting requires energy – you may have to weigh up food gain against the loss of energy and decide when to abandon the hunt in favour of just sitting quietly.

SINGLE LOOP SNARE

- Twist a running loop of wire or smooth rigid nylon into a small eye (or via an overhand knot).
- Feed the free end through the loop and tie to an anchor.
- The loop, whose diameter should match the size of the prey, must close easily.
- Use twigs to hold the loop open.

GROUND-BASED SPRING SNARE

- A simple noose is attached to a strong branch/tree.
- A trigger bar is fitted to a short, straight stake.
- The loop is attached to the trigger bar, which is attached under tension to a pliable bent branch.
- When triggered, the noose will whip up and tighten.

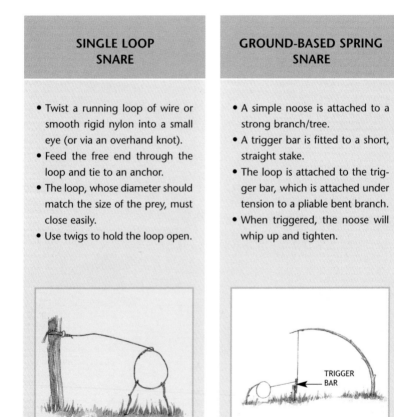

TRIGGER BAR

DEADFALL TRAP

These traps are quite difficult to make, but they are very sensitive, highly effective and definitely worth the effort.

- Attach cord or string to a baited trigger bar.
- When the animal pulls on the bait (or walks into the tensioned cord), it releases the deadfall (a large weight such as a log or rock).

WARNING:
TAKE GREAT CARE WHEN SETTING THESE TRAPS. TRIGGERS NEED TO BE RESPONSIVE, BUT A NUMBER OF HUNTERS HAVE HAD THEIR CREATIONS FALL ON THEM INSTEAD OF THE ANIMAL FOR WHICH IT WAS INTENDED.

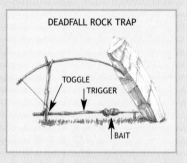

DEADFALL ROCK TRAP

TOGGLE
TRIGGER
BAIT

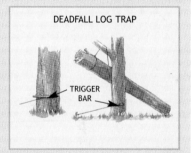

DEADFALL LOG TRAP

TRIGGER BAR

Initially, you may find trapping animals offensive, but in a survival situation you may have to set traps and build snares to catch your food. A hare (such as this), could be a supply of food for a few days.

TIPS FOR TRAPPING

- Patience is key – remember that animals are wary and shrewd; they have to be coaxed or led into traps.
- Set traps along an animal's natural trail.
- Avoid shiny cord or wire for trap construction.
- Try to remove all human scent from the trap and the surrounding area. Wash your hands and then rub them in sand or mud, or in a mixture of sand and the animal's droppings before handling any trap materials.
- You could 'smoke' the trap materials and your body over a fire, although this might discourage certain animals such as monkeys from approaching the trap.
- Once you have identified and know your prey, set as many suitable traps of as many different types as you can manage to conceal in the area.
- Trapping close to the nest or burrow can be tricky – animals are at their most cautious close to their home.
- Be aware of prevailing winds; if your scent is carried downwind it could alert the animal at a crucial time.
- Bait the trap with a suitable food but try to avoid touching it.
- Check traps frequently.

TRACKING AND HUNTING WEAPONS

Tracking and hunting animals is more difficult than snaring. Observe some basic principles, and ensure that you have reliable weapons.

- A slingshot needs practice. Using smooth stones, twirl the sling above your head at speed and release one thong in the intended direction. Make sure you have no-one near you, as your aim will initially be unpredictable and you could cause an injury!

- A spear can be used to bring down large prey such as buck and badgers. It can also be used in fishing (see pp81–85) and as a hiking aid. Fastening a knife or sharpened piece of metal to the front makes the spear more efficient. Practise throwing it from a crouching position without having to stand up as this alerts animals.

- **Catapults** are easily made if you have elasticized material (such as an inner tube or even elastic from clothing) and can be very useful in hunting small game and birds. It is possible to become incredibly accurate with only a small amount of practice.

Hunting Tips

- Use tracks and animal spoor to help locate pathways of movement. Follow this downhill to find watering holes.
- Do not move on the pathways – always keep a distance away or your prey will smell you.
- Choose an appropriate location where you can hide near the track.
- Animals are very alert at watering holes – rather hunt them on their way to or from the water.
- Hunt at first light if you can, or at night when game is more active.
- Move very slowly. Freeze in position if the animal(s) seem to have detected your presence.
- Keep downwind of the prey (keep the wind in your face). By moving quickly in an uphill direction in hilly country in the early morning, you will prevent your scent being carried upwards by thermal currents. You can then hunt downhill without alarming the animals.

You can create your own spear by lashing a knife to the end of a longish branch.

BOW AND ARROW

A bow and arrow is probably the most useful weapon as it can kill at a great distance. It could take a lot of effort to make this weapon but the rewards are considerable.

Making bows

1. Find a hard, springy branch (e.g. young spruce, cedar or eucalyptus) and notch the ends.
2. Fit a loop of tough string to both ends under tension.
3. Lash the loops in place with more cord.
4. Fit an arrow of suitable length.

Making arrows

You need straight wood or perhaps even a piece of a spare tent pole or a suitable vehicle part, such as a section of a fuel or brake line. Notch one end to accommodate the string and sharpen the other end; alternatively, attach a point.

Attach vanes to the end if you have suitable material (e.g. feathers, hard light plastic, tough leaves, cloth or even paper). They will improve the flight of your arrow and can either be lashed in place with cord or stuck on.

Fish are a valuable food source and in addition to their high protein content, also often contain large amounts of fat as well as vitamins and minerals. All freshwater fish and most marine fish are edible, although some are more palatable than others.

Mirror carp is only one of many edible freshwater fish.

It is best to descale and de-bone fish before cooking and eating them although this is not necessary with smaller fish. If the skin of the fish feels slimy, wash the mucus off thoroughly, then rub it with sand to ensure all traces are removed. In some fish the mucus on its skin may be toxic. Certain common marine catfish have poison sacs attached to large spines on their fins, as do tropical species such as trigger fish, stonefish, scorpion fish and zebra fish. Some reef fish, including the porcupine and puffer fish, which both inflate when startled, build up dangerous toxins but not exclusively in their livers. Avoid reef fish that have 'parrot-like' beaks or slimy skins.

Fishing Tips

- Fish are wary creatures; avoid casting a shadow on the surface and sit well back from the bank.
- Fishing is most successful at night or in the early morning.
- Lights (including flaming lamps) often attract fish at night, so can be useful.
- Fish tend to concentrate in calm, deep, shaded pools of water when the weather is hot, and along the edges of sunny patches when it is cool.
- Worms, frogs, crabs and other bait can be found by digging around the edges of a pool or along the riverbank. Once removed from their shells, snails are irresistible to most fish.
- Pre-baiting a likely looking fishing spot by sprinkling bait on the water surface can help to attract fish to the area.
- Live bait attracts fish more effectively.
- It is useful to have some form of net or gaff to land the fish you catch.

USEFUL FISHING EQUIPMENT

- **Rods** are useful to cast over distance, keep shadows off the water and land the fish. A float keeps the hook buoyant and makes it easier to identify a strike.

- **Lures** can be made from brightly coloured materials (feathers, plastic, buttons, cloth or carved wood) and combined with flashy pieces of metal and plastic. Small live insects and invertebrates are good bait. Lures need to be trawled by hand or by boat.

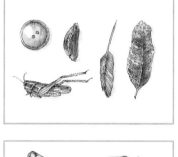

- **Improvised hooks** can be made from a key ring, wire, safety pins, branches and thorns. Attach via a notch in the wood or a closed loop in the metal. File a point or sharpen on stone.

Fish will rise to a variety of lures, spinners and bait. Small live insects and invertebrates are good bait.

FISH TRAPS

Traps are useful as they can be set and left, with you inspecting them at convenient times and intervals. By damming a stream, you can divert the flow into a net or other trap.

Bottle trap
- Cut the neck off a plastic bottle, invert it, then jam it back into the bottle.
- Insert some bait into the main body of the bottle. Small fish cannot find their way out after having swum into the bottle.

Twig trap (lobster trap)
- Create a smaller inner funnel that fits into a larger one by tying sticks together.
- Fill in the spaces with more sticks or with cord to prevent the fish from escaping.
- Close the large funnel at the narrow end and insert the smaller funnel, which ends in a narrow open cone, into the open end of the large one.
- Sharpen the tips of the smaller funnel; it prevents fish from swimming out of the trap.

Sock trap
- Place bait inside a sock.
- Use a loop of wire or a plastic ring to hold it open.
- Place the sock in a stream. Smelly bait (even animal entrails or dung) inside the sock will attract eels.

- **Harpoons** These are useful for catching large fish that come to the surface or when fishing from the bank or in the water. Multi-point harpoons increase your chances of spearing and holding the fish. Because water refracts light, aim lower than the spot where you see the fish.

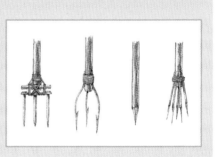

- **Running lines** You are more likely to catch a fish by suspending a series of hooks on lines in a stream or dragging them behind a boat. Placing the hooks at different depths ensures that you cover all levels of fish activity.

- **Ice hole with fishing sticks** Fishing in very cold areas where the water surface has frozen over will entail cutting or knocking a hole through the ice. Be careful that the ice beneath you does not break. Ice fishing is like any other method – it is best to set up many lines and to try different depths and types of bait.

SEA FISHING

Fishing from a boat has distinct advantages when the craft is moving because fish will be attracted by any spinners that turn and flash in the water. Numerous hooks can be placed on one long line, which can be dropped astern. Many fish are also attracted to the shade of the boat and will swim around it for hours.

Turtles, which make an excellent meal, also seem to be attracted to boats.

A net with the right-sized mesh for the size fish you are trying to catch can be used to form a 'fish pool' on the water surface or catch fish at depth. By closing the net rapidly around a school of fish, you may be able to trap quite a substantial amount at once.

A good net size for medium-sized (0.5kg/1lb) fish is to make each mesh hole large enough so that it just fits around an average adult wrist.

CONSTRUCTING A NET

- Suspend strong top rope (or doubled or plaited thin cord) between two posts.
- Tie separate drop-threads of cord to the top rope using cow (girth) hitches.
- Tie together adjacent drop-threads, sequentially, using overhand knots to create the tie-off net.
- Finish by tying double drop-threads to the bottom strong rope using a clove hitch or round turn and two half-hitches.

This net-making method can be used to make a hammock, which is valuable in preventing bed (pressure) sores if you have a disabled or ill group member.

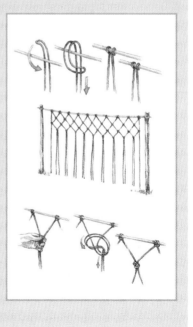

FIRES AND FOOD PREPARATION

Making fires and preparing hot meals without conventional cooking utensils are two skills that should also be practised regularly, just in case of an emergency. It is difficult to make a fire if you do not have matches or a cigarette lighter and some food that you may have found in the environment needs some form of preparation, or it has to be preserved or properly dried to prevent it from spoiling.

As with most survival techniques, improvisation is key. Use whatever suitable materials you have available to create makeshift pots and pans or to build an oven.

Be VERY careful when making a fire in nature! Fires can quickly burn out of control and can destroy everything in its path. In forests, clear the area surrounding the fire or dig a trench around it (fill it with water if you have a good supply), to prevent the fire from spreading.

Apart from providing heat a fire also offers reassurance and is a great morale booster.

FIRES

A fire for warmth, light and cooking is arguably one of the most valuable things in the wilderness. It offers comfort and can make a tremendous difference to a group's physical and mental wellbeing. In a survival situation, fire can often spell the difference between life and death.

Making a fire is simple if you have a cigarette lighter or matches. Waterproof matches are still the best.

If you are fortunate to have some method of making a fire, or have a store of matches, be careful to preserve it. Having to make a fire with minimal materials under difficult conditions such as high wind, cold or rain is an art that deserves some practice.

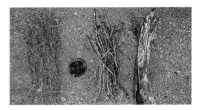

Dry grass, twigs and branches with a dash of petrol are quick fire starters.

Of all disaster scenarios, fires pose the greatest threat to both man and animal. A fire that is allowed to get out of control can turn into a runaway conflagration with horrifying speed and demolish a forest and everything in it in a very short period of time. Be very careful!

FIREMAKING TIPS

- Ensure that there is adequate ventilation – fires produce a lot of harmful gases, and also consume oxygen.
- If building a fire in the midst of vegetation, clear an area of at least 2m (6ft) around the fire – more if there is a strong wind, and if the surrounding vegetation is particularly dry.
- Take care not to make the fire too close to overhanging branches.
- Always make sure that the embers have died down completely before leaving the area. This is especially true of deep embers that may smoulder for days.
- Build an earth bank or a circle of stones around the fire to contain it, or dig a trench around it.
- For wet or snow-covered ground, light the fire on a platform of green logs or place it on a detached part of a vehicle.

Firemaking material

- **Tinder:** This is needed to start a fire. Any dry, fine, combustible material such as paper, moss, tree bark, dry leaves, grass, animal dung or fungi will allow a spark to take. It may be necessary to crush or grind the material first to make it fine enough to flare easily.

- **Kindling:** Small leaves, sticks and pieces of dry bark form the next additive to the fire once the kindling has caught. Add these slowly and carefully until a clear flame is visible.

- **Main fuel:** Add fuel progressively to avoid smothering the fire. Small sticks need to go on first, then large branches or logs as the fire takes. Greenish wood or wet fuel can be dried out next to a fire to provide the next load of fuel.

Alternative fuels

Many substances will burn, particularly fuels, plastic, rubber and cloth. Some of these, particularly plastics, give off noxious gases. Use them only as a last resort and ensure the fire is lit in a well-ventilated area.

Oil and petrol can be persuaded to burn more slowly by pouring them into a container of sand and lighting them. Oils and diesel fuel burn more readily when mixed with petrol. Hydraulic fluid and pure antifreeze are also flammable.

A useful way of getting a 'lazy' fire to start is by flaming it with an aerosol can. Many aerosol propellants and contents burn well. However, be careful – if used for too long the nozzle can get hot enough to melt.

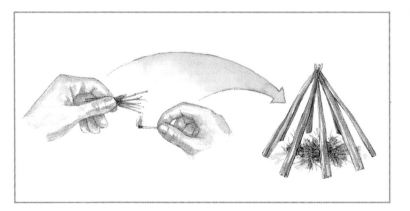

Light a bundle of dry tinder beneath a pyramid of branches, which will eventually burn from the build-up of heat.

Lighting a fire without matches or lighters

The following methods are worth trying, although none are quite as easy as they sound.

- Strong sunlight focused through a magnifying glass, or even fairly strong glasses, can start a fire. Binocular and camera lenses can provide a number of useful lenses if broken open.
- Flintstones generate sparks when they are struck against one another, or with a hard piece of steel. Sparks should be directed into a bed of very fine, dry tinder.
- Magnesium blocks available from outdoor stores, are highly inflammable. The scrapings from these blocks provide superb tinder.

- A car or other large battery (even lamp batteries) can produce sufficient sparks to light a fire. Beware, as this depletes a battery and can cause it to heat up. If you are using a car battery, remove it from the vehicle first.
- A small amount of petrol poured on a cloth lights very easily. Be sure not to use too much, and stand well

A blade struck against a rock creates sparks that can be directed onto bone-dry tinder to start a fire.

back when igniting the piece of cloth.
- You are unlikely to have chemicals available, but your survival kit may contain potassium permanganate. You should also have sugar, while glycerine is found in many first-aid kits. Mix the sugar and potassium permanganate (one part sugar to eight or nine parts of potassium permanganate), then add the hand-warmed glycerine. It should flare up after a while. You may even be able to ignite this mixture without glycerine, by grinding it between two rocks.

Apart from the normal pyramid fire (see p89), you can build fires that make more efficient use of available fuel, and are less hazardous.

- **Star fires** take their name from the circular arrangement of logs (big ones work best) that point to a central fire. The logs are pushed inward as more fuel is needed. Rocks can be placed in the spaces between the logs to provide cooking platforms and to hold the logs in place. One or more reflector shields will help you to direct warmth to you or the group.

NOTE: ROCKS MAY SPLIT OR CRACK IN FIRE, PARTICULARLY WET OR POROUS ONES. BEWARE OF FLYING PIECES OF ROCK: THEY CAN CAUSE SERIOUS INJURY.

- A **trench or pit fire** is placed in a hole to shelter it from strong wind. This reduces the danger of flying sparks. As this method diminishes ventilation to the fire, it is best to place a layer of fairly large rocks on the bottom and build the fire on top of them.

- A **tin, or 'hobo', fire** uses a good-sized tin, with a few holes knocked in underneath and around the lower end to form a very fuel-efficient stove. It is best to cut a panel at the base, which can be folded back to regulate air supply and allow for the insertion of fuel. Various options exist for the top – one entails punching holes in the top to allow anything placed on it to cook slowly. You can also cut a single large hole to accommodate your pot, and build the fire on stable stones placed inside for improved air circulation.

FOOD PREPARATION AND PRESERVATION

Most food needs some preparation to make it more palatable or to remove poisonous or harmful sections. In the case of animals, skin, fur, feathers, scales and bones often need to be removed. Larger animals are best skinned hanging up, preferably from the head as this makes it easier to remove the internal organs. A good skinning knife has a sharp blade, but a rounded end – this enables one to separate the skin from the underlying tissues without cutting it. Once the separation has started, skin can often be peeled off by hand.

In a true survival situation, you would eat parts of animals that would usually be thrown away. In fact, very little cannot be eaten.

In many cases, food does not actually need cooking and the process actually

Lemons, limes or similar, together with salt if available, make good pickling fluids that help to preserve vital foods. In general, the stronger the solution, the better the preservation.

destroys many vital nutrients such as vitamin C which our bodies require.

On the other hand, circumstances might force you to eat food raw – do this with the knowledge that our bodies are actually biologically adapted to a diet of primarily raw foodstuffs.

If you need to move from a location where you have built up a store of food, you will need to take supplies with you. Large, dry gourds and thick pieces of bamboo can serve as carrying containers. Seal openings with beeswax or a plastic bag. Clay can also be used, but it cracks easily when it gets dry and could contaminate the food in the container. Mix thin pieces of bark or grass into the clay to bind it.

If you have dried or smoked meat, wrap it in large leaves, but open and check for mould regularly.

Fish or meat strips can be dried on this improvised drying rack.

Methods of preservation

To prevent food from spoiling, it must be properly dried or preserved.

- The citric acids of limes and lemons are useful to pickle fish, meat, and even vegetables. Use a lot of juice with equal parts of water.
- A strong salt solution can be used to pickle foods. When a raw potato, tuber, egg or onion begins to float in a salt solution, it indicates that the brine is strong enough to use as a preservative.

- Preserve fruits and some vegetables by cutting them into thin slices before they are sun-dried or even smoked.
- Lichens and seaweed need to be boiled before drying. Grind them to a powder, and this can be used to add flavouring to soups and stews.
- Nuts and grain cereals easily turn mouldy. Smoke or sun-dry them (or dry them directly on hot rocks) before storing them, preferably in a sealed watertight container.

FOOD PREPARATION TIPS

- Offal (lungs, liver, heart, kidneys, etc.) is not easy to preserve and should be eaten first. Lungs have little nutritional value and can be used as bait.
- Meat and fish can be preserved by boiling, smoking or drying.
- When smoking meat, one of the simplest ways of making a 'smokehouse' is to close off the sides of a tripod stand made over an open fire.
- The smoking process requires lots of smoke and a slow-burning low fire. Avoid wood with a lot of resin or a very strong smell, as this may make the meat inedible.
- Cut meat to be smoked or sun-dried into very thin strips, remove the fat, and then string or spear it onto sticks or racks.
- It can take many hours (or days) to smoke meat thoroughly to ensure that it is dry but still retains a small amount of moisture.
- Sun-drying needs time and can only be attempted in warm, dry climates. If you have salt available, rub this into the meat to aid preservation. However, bear in mind that this could make you more thirsty later.
- Watch for flies – they could lay maggots in the meat.

FOOD FROM INVERTEBRATES

The best and easiest protein and general food sources often go unnoticed for a long time in survival situations simply because the survivors are not attuned to eating them.

Invertebrates – the so-called 'lower life forms' – are abundant in most parts of the world and have value as a nutritional food source.

Termites are plentiful and nutritious.

TIPS FOR THE COLLECTION AND USE OF INVERTEBRATES

- Be on the lookout for spiders, scorpions and centipedes, many of which can give you a nasty (or even fatal) bite or sting. Avoid spiders and centipedes as a food source, although scorpions can be eaten once their tail (and hence the sting) has been removed.
- Avoid brightly coloured invertebrates and snails, they are often poisonous.
- Certain cone-shell snails can inject a small dart, which has been known to cause serious nerve damage and even death. Avoid these conids.
- Hornets, wasps and bees can provide a good meal. Nests contain larvae and pupae – tasty, nutritious food – and of course bees make honey. Smoke can make bees drowsy, kill them, or drive them off the nest, but if there's not enough smoke it can also drive them into a frenzy and they will attack mercilessly, so be careful. Anyone allergic to bee stings must be very cautious.
- When dealing with bees, cover your entire body and head with thick, sting-proof clothing, or swaddle a sleeping bag or similar around yourself. Bees are inactive at night so this is the best time to try to extract honey from a hive with the aid of copious smoke.
- Most small invertebrates can be eaten raw and offer better food value when uncooked. To make them more palatable, they can be boiled, roasted on hot stones or directly on a fire. Remove stings, wings, legs, hairs on caterpillars (can be singed off in a flame), and the hard outer casings of beetles or larvae.

Marine invertebrates

Nearly every coastline offers a rich harvest of food. Shelled creatures and most marine invertebrates are edible. If you are marooned at the seaside, it is unlikely that food would be a major concern. Be on the lookout for small breathing holes in the sand, which often indicate the presence of sea slugs and sand mussels.

In need, even this small crab will make a welcome meal for a hungry survivor.

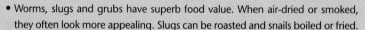

- Worms, slugs and grubs have superb food value. When air-dried or smoked, they often look more appealing. Slugs can be roasted and snails boiled or fried.
- Insects, particularly small ones, can be dried and crushed to form a paste. This can be used as an additive to soups and stews. Locusts and grasshoppers are common in all countries – they are deservedly regarded as a delicacy by many African tribes.
- Termites are an excellent food source. Their large mounds, which can be broken open to yield both mature adults and grubs, are easily spotted. After heavy rains, termites perform mating flights and can be easily gathered in large quantities. They can be eaten raw, roasted or fried. Dried and ground they make a very nutritious and easily transportable food supplement.
- A pit trap consisting of a container (e.g. a cup) in a hole, with a log or stone to cover it, can be effective in catching insects. Placing sweetened water, honey, fruit or other sweet substance in the container will act as an additional attraction.

A simple insect pit trap

TIPS ON CATCHING MARINE CREATURES

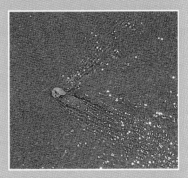

- You can usually find shellfish by digging down into the sand close to the tide line as they often come closer to the surface at night. A distinctive V-shape as the water runs back in the shallows (right) signals their presence. Shellfish can move back down their burrows rapidly, so dig quickly while flicking the wet sand aside.

- Salt, vinegar or even lemon juice can provoke shellfish and burrowing worms and prawns to come to the surface.

- As filter feeders, shellfish can build up dangerous quantities of pollutants (such as lead and mercury salts) as well as the red-tide diatoms. Be aware of this. Shellfish should be boiled and eaten soon after harvesting. Leftovers are best discarded.

- Crabs (below) and crayfish, or lobsters, must be thoroughly cleaned. Always remove the gills and stomach before eating. Remember that the claws contain good amounts of meat.

- Red bait can be collected from the rocks at low tide. The inside can be eaten, as can the insides of sea urchins and starfish.

- Avoid jellyfish, sea anemones (below right) and coral. They have little nutritional value and their stinging cells can contain poisons.

PREPARING HOT MEALS

Cooked foods are more palatable, and the heat will eliminate potentially harmful bacteria and parasites. Warmth obtained from hot food can make a critical difference to body temperature in very cold conditions.

Under normal conditions, outdoor cooking can be an art and a pleasure. Under extreme circumstances, it may become a desperate and onerous duty, albeit an essential one.

If you do not have conventional cooking utensils, you will have to devise makeshift pots and pans from tin cans, hubcaps, parts of vehicles, gourds and bamboo; you will also have to carve wooden spoons, make twig forks and a branch pot holder.

- **Simple spit:** is useful for suspending cooking pots, as well as whole carcasses, and for drying clothes. Using heavily branched sticks for the

Use a tray to catch the fat dripping off a spit roast.

upright allows you to adjust the height of the spit by digging the branch stumps deeper into the earth.

- **A cantilever pot holder:** allows the pot to be swung off the fire for stirring or inspection (see p98). The support stick has to be very stable.

- **Hot rocks:** can either be heated up in a fire and removed when needed, or the fire can be made on a bed of rocks. When the fire has burnt out, the rocks can be swept clean, and the food cooked on top of them.

Rocks retain heat well and can be used to slow-cook food.

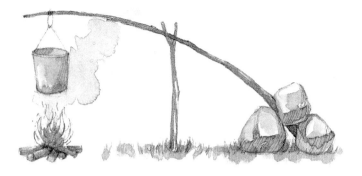

A cantilever-style pot holder needs a strong branch.

- **Bed of coals:** is a useful method if you have no container at all. You can wrap food in a suitably large, nonpoisonous leaf (for edibility test, see p71). Then plaster the leaf with mud and place this 'mud sandwich' on the bed of coals, layering more coals on top if possible. This method is a slow but effective way of cooking most meals.

- **Yukon oven:** it is worth the effort to build one of these if you are going to be at a site for a long period of time.

  First hollow out a pit with an extra channel on one side that will allow you to add fuel. Build a fire in the pit, arrange stones around it in a circle and pack them with clay, adding further layers of rock to form a 'chimney'. The top of the chimney is used as a cooking hole and platform. You can add fuel to the fire from the hole left at the side.

A deserted termite mound can be used as a chimney, and the base then hollowed out as a place for the fire.

Variations of the above include the any size or type of metal box with a lid, which can be built into the side of the Yukon oven to make it more versatile and even more effective. You can even bake bread in it.

CROSS SECTION

Yukon ovens use the convection principle.

Camping stoves

- Standard camping gas stoves are the best for lightweight camping trips. They do not burn well at altitude on their normal butane fuel, but have been used with special propane-butane mixes right up to the highest camps on Mount Everest. They light easily with a controllable flame. Cartridges must be empty before they are removed (never throw them into a fire as they can explode). Do not change cylinders in the vicinity of open flames.

- Gas stoves with removable cartridges can be stored and carried separately from the cartridge, which can also be used on a matching gas lamp when it is not needed for the stove.

  The propane-butane fuel mixture is readily available, and produces more heat. Many fuels found in fuel bottles are poisonous, and all are highly inflammable. The best containers are aluminium bottles with screw-on lids fitted with appropriate rubber or plastic washers. Ensure that fuel bottles are distinctively marked to avoid confusing them with water bottles. If possible, use a permanent marker to label them correctly (add a warning symbol). Alternatively, paste a clearly written label on the container and cover it with transparent plastic.

- Meths stoves use methylated spirits or ethanol (known as 'cooking alcohol'

in many parts of the world). Most of the available models come as compact fold-up units, complete with kettle, pots and windscreen.

- Multi-fuel stoves run on petrol, benzene, paraffin and even raw alcohol.

  Multi-fuel stoves tend to be noisy and difficult to light; they are also subject to fits of temper (flare-ups, blocked jets), but are efficient and allow users to burn a variety or even a mixture of fuel. Do not use these stoves in tents or other confined spaces as the pressurizing system is not always completely reliable.

  Most multi-fuel stoves work well at altitude, but their irregularity counts against them at extreme altitude, where you may be feeling sluggish and slow to react to their unpredictability.

An aluminium set comprising gas burner, stove and flask.

NAVIGATION

Having the knowledge of your current position and terrain will play an important role in determining the level of certainty regarding your movements in a survival situation. Having a map, a Global Positioning System (GPS) receiver and compass, knowing your location and where you would find some civilization would be ideal if you find yourself in such a situation.

Maps are useful as they indicate distance, direction, special features and geographical landmarks. It is also wise to practise using a compass – having the instrument and not being able to read it is of no use in an emergency situation. Once you are able to orientate your map and compass to your current location, finding your way will become less difficult.

Proficiency in map-reading and navigational skills will stand you in good stead when travelling through unfamiliar territory.

NAVIGATION

If in unknown territory, finding your way is best achieved with a map and a compass or GPS, which should be readily available in your kit.

USING MAPS

- **Direction via north–south (N–S) lines** (or grid lines). Once a map is orientated, then natural features on the map such as rivers, hills and valleys should match what you see on the ground.
- **Distance via the scale of the map.**
Maps have different scales and thus varying degrees of accuracy. A hiking map usually has a scale from 1:25,000 to 1:50,000 (e.g. at a scale of 1:50,000, for every cm you measure on the map, there are 50,000cm in reality on the ground). This means 1cm on a map represents 500m; 1in represents 50,000in. Detailed hiking 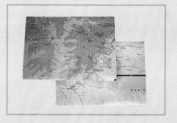 maps of, say, 1:10,000 (1cm = 100m or 0.4in = 328ft) show more features but cover a more restricted area. Aeronautical charts, on the other hand, are usually 1:250,000 and give you a good idea of surrounding areas, but don't provide too much detail.
- **Heights, via contour lines.** These also give an indication of the slope or gradient and spot heights (e.g. peak heights). The contour interval is the vertical height difference represented by each line, usually about 10–20m (40–80ft). The closer together the contour lines, the steeper the slope. Take careful note of slope angles. A cliff or steep drop-off is indicated by many contour lines that virtually meet.
- **Special features and geographical landmarks** i.e lakes, rivers, cliffs, roads, buildings and vegetation.

Orientating your map

A map is only really of value if you can match it to your present position and the surrounding terrain. This will give you a better idea of where you are and the direction you need to take when you decide to make a move. The first objective is thus to orientate your map to the terrain and to north.

ORIENTATION VIA TERRAIN

If you know exactly or even roughly where you are and visibility is good, then you can often line up your map with the help of prominent features such as hills, peaks, rivers or lakes. Study the map carefully, then turn it until the features shown by contours and conventional signs/map symbols match the terrain you are in.

ORIENTATION VIA COMPASS

The easiest way to line up a map is by using a compass or some other method of finding north. It is advisable to do this anyway, since lining up the map via the terrain only could be misleading. The most suitable compass for walking and map-reading is the Silva type, which is fairly inexpensive, robust, and easy to use.

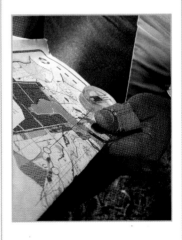

Magnetic north and true north

The map must be lined up with north: remember that maps show true north on their N–S lines. This differs from magnetic north (shown by the compass) by a varying number of degrees according to where you are on the earth. (The magnetic north pole is not exactly at the earth's geographical, or true north pole.) This difference is known as magnetic variation (or magnetic declination).

The map should have a legend giving magnetic north as: e.g. 'magnetic variation (or 'declination') 15 degrees east'. This means that the magnetic pole actually lies 15 degrees east (to the right) of true north in the area covered by that map; therefore the compass reading is 'inaccurate' by 15 degrees east (right) of true north.

Rotate the map 15 degrees westwards (left, or anticlockwise) from the compass north (magnetic north) to line up on true north, so it matches up exactly with the terrain as you see it (see diagram above). Many maps have three arrows to show different variations: magnetic north, true north and grid north.

The latter system is favoured by the military and by some countries including England and several Western European countries. However, the difference between grid and true north is so small as to be insignificant for any non-military purposes, so grid north lines can be taken as true north.

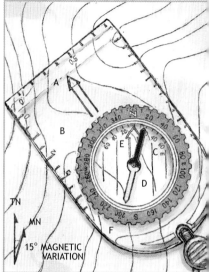

The silva-type compass – A: direction of travel arrow; B: base plate; C: red magnetic (north) needle; D: white (south) needle; E: red north (0°) indicator; F: rotating bezel.

Using the map only

Once the map is orientated, you can use it to establish your exact position. You are then able to plot your most suitable pathway e.g. 'down the valley on our east, over the neck, down the southwards ridge to the road'. Simply follow your selected route using the features shown on the map to guide you, while continuing to keep a careful eye on where you are on the map by matching the features surrounding you on the ground.

At night or in poor weather conditions you may have to depend on a combination of map and compass by which to travel. The compass bearing will give you the direction. Bearings run from 0° (north) via 90° (east) through 180° (south) and 270° (west), with the full circle being at 360° (north again).

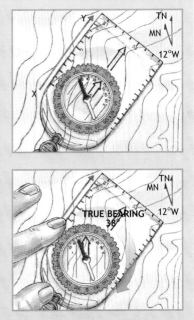

A. First establish precisely where you are on the map – your present position (X), then select your destination on the map (Y). Place the compass so that the edge of the base plate (and the direction of the travel arrow) run from X to your destination Y.

B. Rotate the bezel so that the north indicator on the bezel lines up with the north–south lines (pointing to true north) on the map. Read the figures where the base line of the direction of travel arrow meets the bezel. This is known as your grid or true bearing. Convert this to magnetic (compass) bearing by adding or subtracting (as given on the map). If the variation is given as: 12° west, add this to the grid or true bearing. If it is given as: 12° east, subtract it from the bearing; e.g. for a declination of 12° W on a map (true) bearing of 38°, add 12° declination to give a final 50° magnetic (compass) bearing. Set this last bearing by turning the bezel to 50° to line up with the base of the travel arrow on the compass.

C. Hold the compass level so that the needle swings freely. Rotate your body until the red north point lines up with the north indicator on the bezel. The direction-of-travel arrow points in the direction you must head (i.e. true bearing 38°, plus 12° W magnetic variation, to give an adjusted direction of 50°). In brief, the magnetic compass needle always points to magnetic north – and you have just set on your compass, using the direction-of-travel arrow, the way you should be heading. Provided you keep the magnetic needle lined up with the north indicator arrow on the bezel, and follow the direction-of-travel arrow, you will safely be heading towards your destination.

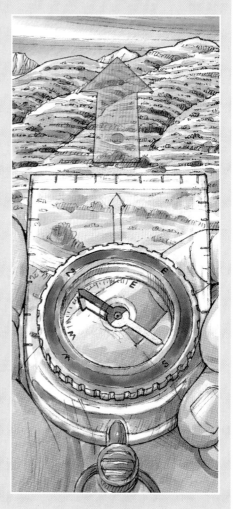

FINDING DIRECTION WITHOUT A COMPASS

If you have a compass or can improvise one, then locating north is fairly easy, but bear in mind that magnetic deviation may vary in different world regions. If you don't have a commercial compass available, there are several ways of finding direction by using natural features.

THE SUN

The sun rises roughly in the east and sets roughly in the west. There is quite a bit of seasonal variation due to the tilt of the earth on its axis. If you are in the Northern Hemisphere, the sun is due south when at its highest point in the sky. The opposite concept will thus hold true for the Southern Hemisphere.

A Shadow Stick can be used to find both your direction and the time of day.

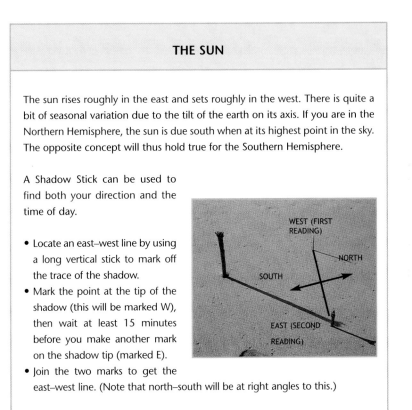

- Locate an east–west line by using a long vertical stick to mark off the trace of the shadow.
- Mark the point at the tip of the shadow (this will be marked W), then wait at least 15 minutes before you make another mark on the shadow tip (marked E).
- Join the two marks to get the east–west line. (Note that north–south will be at right angles to this.)

The longer the time interval, the more accurate the line will be. Remember that the shadow moves clockwise (west to east) in the Northern Hemisphere and anticlockwise (east to west) in the Southern Hemisphere. The diagram above shows a Northern Hemisphere reading.

NORTHERN HEMISPHERE

Stars appear to 'move' across the sky because of the rotation of the earth. As the north, or pole star is at the axis of rotation it 'stands still' and can thus be used to find north in the Northern Hemisphere. If location is a problem, then use the distinctive Big Dipper and the position of the Milky Way to identify the pole star.

North star

In the Northern Hemisphere, the 'stationary' pole star (Polaris) – in the constellation known as Ursa Minor (the Lesser Bear) – is located by extending a line from the two bright stars that form the left-hand side of the Big Dipper's bowl (in the constellation Ursa Major, or the Great Bear). However, above 60–65° north latitude, Polaris is too high in the sky to be an accurate guide to north.

SOUTHERN HEMISPHERE

It helps to get your bearings by finding south. When you have found the conspicuous Southern Cross and its two pointers, use an imaginary line to extend the long axis of the cross. Next take a line that bisects the pointers and extend it. Where these two imaginary lines meet is the Celestial South Pole. Drop a line straight down to the horizon to give true south.

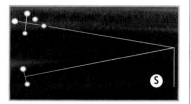

Southern Cross

PLANTS AND NATURAL FEATURES

If it is cloudy or heavily overcast, various other natural features can be useful in confirming your sun sighting or star sighting at night.

- **River flow:** If you know the principal direction in which a major river flows in the area in which you find yourself, this would help to confirm direction. Remember, however, that many rivers meander a good deal.
- **Lichens and moss:** These grow in greatest profusion on the shaded side of trees – in the Southern Hemisphere this would be the south side, while it would be the north side in the Northern hemisphere.

- **Trees and flowers:** In older trees, the annual growth rings (which can be seen on a tree stump) are larger on the side that faces the Equator.
- **Flowers:** These mostly face the main course of the sun to flower better – this would be north for the Southern Hemisphere and vice versa.

BIRDS AND INSECTS

The African Weaver bird, which is found predominantly south of the Equator, builds its nest on the west side of trees.

In many regions, termites build their characteristic mound nests orientated north to south in order to maximize shade in the heat of day.

Improvised compass

If you need a compass to navigate but do not have one, you might be able to create a compass needle from a sliver of iron or steel, or a razor blade, using one of several methods.

- A reasonably strong battery (such as one used for a car or a series of lamp cells that have been connected up) can give a strong enough current to magnetize steel. The harder the metal (e.g. a tempered steel  needle) and the tighter the coil, the longer the magnetism will last. Continually make and break contact quite a few times; this will help fortify the magnetism.

- By repeatedly stroking a needle in one direction on silk (or even certain synthetic fabrics), it will become magnetized. Remagnetize regularly as the magnetism in your makeshift compass needle diminishes with time.

  - If you have a magnet, you can use it directly as a north indicator, or if it is too large for this purpose, use it to magnetize a smaller piece of metal. Magnets can be sourced from parts of many car generators and alternators as well as in some radio loudspeakers and toy motors.

  - After you have magnetized the metal it must be allowed to swing freely. This is done by either floating it on water or suspending it from a very light thread.

  - As the needle indicates only a north–south line and there is no indication on which is north and which is south, there are, however, other methods (see p103) to decide which end of your improvised compass needle points north.

The capabilities of a satellite navigation (GPS) device – held here by a traveller wearing a mask to protect his face against a blizzard – are put to good use in a featureless snow-filled landscape.

GLOBAL POSITIONING SYSTEM AND ALTIMETERS

Modern tools such as wrist compasses and altimeters (sophisticated watches that also indicate direction, air pressure and altitude above sea level), as well as Global Positioning System (GPS) devices can be extremely valuable in locating position and movement. The GPS uses over two dozen permanently positioned satellites in the earth's orbit to establish the location of your portable GPS receiver via the triangulation

Technology in the form of GPS has greatly improved travel for modern adventurers.

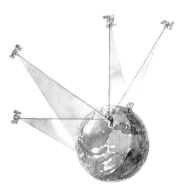

The triangulation of radio signals activated by satellite is valuable as it can instantaneously establish the precise location of the GPS device in three dimensions – giving latitude, longitude and altitude. It also tracks any changes in position, thus allowing survivors who may have to move to update their location to search teams.

of radio signals. The coordinates of your position (where you are on the surface of the earth in terms of latitude – east and west – and longitude – north and south) will appear on the GPS as a set of six to twelve figures known as the grid reference. For example, '1655E2235N' means that your position is 16° and 55 minutes east, and 22° and 35 minutes north. This can help to locate your exact position on a map and may also be used to send positional information to rescuers via radio or cellular (mobile) phone.

Some GPS devices also give altitude, barometric trends (for weather prediction), plot the course you have been moving or perform the same direction-of-travel functions as a compass. Perhaps their biggest limitation is that of battery power – be conservative in your use of such devices, because when they run out, they are of no further use.

MAKING A MOVE

People who find themselves in a predicament are generally tempted to immediately react, rush off to look for rescue, or try to find their own way out of the circumstances. Before embarking on any course of action, sit down and take careful stock of your predicament. Immediately after your situation has occurred, you and the members of your group may still be in a state of shock, and decisions taken hastily or at an early stage may not necessarily be the best ones. Movement should be seen as the last resort unless there is a clear-cut route toward help and rescue, or rescuers are unlikely to find you easily in your current location.

There is a fine balance between deciding to wait for possible rescue or resolving to keep moving and risk the endangerment of any member of the group.

PREPARING TO MOVE

If moving seems inevitable, then make sure that the group is as well equipped as possible and that you have taken everything that might be of use. This applies particularly to any items that may be useful in erecting quick forms of shelter. If you are abandoning a vehicle, first ensure that all possible items of survival value have been taken.

Depending on the terrain, it may be easier to carry supplies or move injured people by creating a sledge or some form of backpack. The simplest option is to tie clothes or cloth into a sausage-shaped pack or a pouch that can also be useful if you need to move small children.

Ensure that all members of the group know the intended route in case someone gets lost.

Before moving on, remember to leave some clear form of message for rescuers, indicating your direction of travel and time of departure, particularly if you are abandoning a vehicle.

The choice between moving or staying put is sometimes a difficult one. Of all the actions taken in a disaster situation, this requires the most careful analysis. Both courses of action may have advantages and disadvantages; both may encompass elements of risk.

CHECKLIST – MOVING VS. STAYING

- What type of situation are you in? If a vehicle is involved (e.g. a car, ship or aeroplane) it might be far easier for searchers to spot it than a group or individual on foot.
- Is anyone likely to know your present location? Are you still on your scheduled route or have you moved far off the original route plan? Do you know where you are relative to your original route, or to a road, railway or some form of civilization? If you left the area, would you simply be heading off blindly in an unknown direction?
- How well do you know your location? If you don't know the area, can you establish whether the nature of the terrain is suitable to the skills of the group? Are the potential hazards such that movement is an unwise option?
- If there are injured group members, how serious are their injuries? How easily can they be moved? Should victims be moved at all?
- What is your food, water and equipment stock? How long do you estimate your current provisions will last?
- How long do you think it would take before someone realizes you are missing and reacts accordingly? What is your estimated time of arrival and by how long has it been exceeded?
- What are your chances of being found or rescued? Do you have a realistic idea of how long it would take to be found if someone did launch a rescue operation?
- Do you or your group have any special needs? Do any of your group members need special medication (e.g. for chronic conditions such as diabetes or hypertension)?
- Is splitting the group a viable option? Would it be feasible to send some members for help and leave the rest of the group behind?

ADVANTAGES OF STAYING

- Movement requires more energy – conserving energy allows your food supplies to last longer.
- Injured, old or sick members of the group will not be exposed to the stress or rigours of having to move.
- The group can plan and implement some signals to alert rescuers, such as burning tyres to make smoke.
- It provides the opportunity to make a more permanent shelter.
- The risks are known – hiking off into unfamiliar terrain may expose you to greater hazards.

ADVANTAGES OF MOVING

- It might be psychologically better for the group to take action than to wait things out.
- Good shelter, food and water might be easier to obtain at a different location.
- If rescue is unlikely for some time and resources are insufficient, then movement can save the day.
- If camp is made in one area for an extended period, hygiene might deteriorate, making sanitary conditions more hazardous.
- If at high altitude, it might be necessary to descend to maintain the health of the group.

It is important to keep the group together when moving. This may be difficult, especially if there are small children in the group.

GROUP MOVEMENT PATTERNS

It is best to keep a group together when moving, although large discrepancies in age or fitness, or injured members could make it difficult. Moving is made even more difficult in fog, falling snow, rain or mist, or when moving at night. The most sensible option is to fully explain the implications of having to search for members who have split up or gone missing.

- A scout (or two) should go slightly ahead of the other members to find the most suitable path.
- Most of the members should follow him/her with the leader in the group.
- Enlist a responsible person as the 'tail-end-Charlie' to ensure that no stragglers fall behind.
- The scouts should not lose visual or auditory touch with the group.
- Each group member should keep in constant contact with the person behind and in front of him/her.
- It is the leader's responsibility to stop for regular checks and head counts.
- Every member should know what action to take in the event of being separated from the group.
- If a lost person is certain of the direction from which he or she has come, the most sensible strategy would be to retrace his or her steps slowly, stopping regularly to call and listen for any responses from the group.

In misty or overcast conditions, it is imperative for members of the group to remain within sight of one another.

- Have a whistle; it improves the chances of locating someone who is lost.

There is an exception to the rule of splitting a group – when a small group of physically fit members who are able to move quickly, forms part of a larger, slower group. The small group can then act as a scouting party and also focus on finding food, water and shelter or cutting a path for the slower group.

FACILITATING MOVEMENT

'Short roping' is a useful technique and may be an option for people who find it difficult to move over downhill terrain.

- A strong, fit member uses a 'tether' or leash to support a less able person.
- The guide holds the rope tightly to provide support when the person being held needs it.
- The guide remains above and slightly to one side of the person if possible.
- If the rope is quite long, the guide can coil the excess around his body and use it to assist someone up or down larger drops.
- With some practice, short roping can greatly speed up group movement

while providing support to people who would otherwise feel uneasy on difficult terrain.

Route markers

Routes can be marked by cutting marks into trees, tying knots in grass, placing sticks or stones in patterns on the ground or tying pieces of material to prominent natural features i.e. large rocks or trees.

Remember that what you might think is an obvious marker might not be so clear to those who are following, especially if they are tired and sick, or it is raining or snowing. Move back and then up to your marker(s) to check whether it is clearly visible.

In bad visibility becoming separated is a real threat. Loop a rope around the waist of the leading person and link it to one or more companions.

A good commercial backpack has a well-padded hip belt and broad, comfortable shoulder straps. An internal frame makes the pack lighter and more streamlined. Side and top pouches make it possible to pack frequently used items and emergency gear (i.e. first-aid kits) where they are easily accessible.

No matter how well made, backpacks are seldom truly waterproof, therefore it is best to wrap everything in several strong plastic bags. These bags have many other uses in normal camping and emergencies and are thus never a waste.

A smallish pack is suitable for women or children on weekend hikes as its padded hip belt and shoulder straps ensure comfortable carrying.

This compact day pack is best for carrying the essentials on a short hike. The hip belt is only slightly padded and offers little support for the load.

MAKESHIFT BACKPACKS

If you don't have a commercially made pack you will have to create your own. This will free your hands for scrambling, pushing vegetation aside, carrying a stretcher or sled, and helping others.

- Trim a forked or y-shaped branch to create a frame (see illustration above right).
- Wrap the gear into a groundsheet or large piece of clothing and tie it to the frame.
- Wrap any spare material around the frame to pad it and avoid bruising your back and hips.
- The broader you can make the shoulder straps of your pack, the better.

The Hudson Bay Pack (see illustration below) is another handy way of slinging goods across your back and entails tying gear into a piece of cloth (preferably waterproof).

- Tie fist-sized stones or similar objects into the diagonally opposite corners of a square cloth (about 1 x 1m; 3 x 3ft) with strong cord or bark.
- Roll your goods in the cloth, then tie the cloth up and lay the bundle across your back or fasten it around your waist.

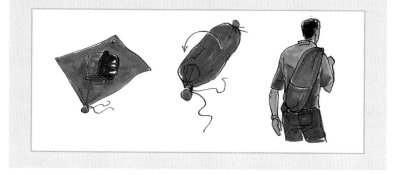

CREATING SLEDS AND CARRYING FRAMES

Two-toed sled (travois): This is the easiest and most basic sled to create.

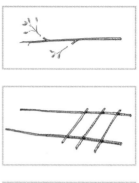

- Join any two fairly long branches or even pack frames to create two runners that simply drag on the ground.
- Join the two runners by using items of clothing (i.e. put the runners through the sleeves of shirts or jackets) or lash on additional smaller branches.

- One or more people can pick up the rear when crossing rough terrain.

The disadvantage is that the dragging toes of the sled can cut deeply into the substrate, making it quite cumbersome to pull. If moving across snow, making small flat runners will improve the sled's mobility.

Curved runner sledge: This version takes more time and effort to make, but is much easier to move than the simple sled. It is far superior on snow, ice or smooth ground and can be dragged on long lines if necessary.

- Create a suitable curve to the sledge by pulling up the two main runners, bracing them with sticks or cord pulled from the tips towards the back.
- If travelling down a steep incline, a person can use a rope, if you have one, to brake the sledge from the back.

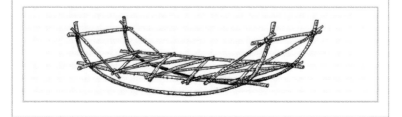

MOVEMENT AT NIGHT

Movement at night should only be undertaken if there is good and sound reason for it. There are situations where it is unavoidable – in the case of medical emergencies, in desert areas where it is inadvisable to travel during the day, and perhaps on snow or glaciers, which become safer when they harden at night.

Disadvantages of moving at night:
- It is difficult to stay orientated without clear landmarks.
- The stars can be a useful aid but it is difficult to keep them in sight and move simultaneously.
- You are unable to anticipate obstacles and steep drop-offs.
- It can be difficult to ensure that the group stays together.

If there are no effective lamps or ones with limited battery power, wait a while before starting out, as one's night vision takes over half an hour to develop fully.

Ways of preserving night vision
- Use a red filter over a lamp when reading a map. Ask one person to do this.
- Preserve 50 per cent of your night vision by using only one eye when the light is on; keep the other tightly shut.
- Focus slightly to one side of the object you are viewing – the rods (the eye's vision cells that see in black and white and are best for night vision) are located off-centre.
- Slowly scan your eyes in a circular fashion to get a better night image of an object.

There are quite a few disadvantages to moving at night, however, in the case of an emergency it may be unavoidable.

Route retention

In the dark, one way of maintaining direction is to use the Triplet Method (see illustration below).

- First establish the direction of travel. The 'leader' sets the 'aimer' off, stopping him/her at a reasonable distance along the line of travel.

- The 'target' person is then sent past the aimer until he reaches the limits of the leader's range of vision; the leader positions him in line with the aimer.
- The leader moves up to the aimer, the target person becomes the new aimer, and the original aimer moves up as the new target.

Phase 1 establishes the line.

Phase 2 shows people leapfrogging the line.

Linking hands is effective provided the river crossing is not too hazardous.

CROSSING RIVERS

Rivers can constitute a major barrier for a person or group, especially if they are tired, cold and disorientated. It is all too easy to underestimate the power of a river and find yourself in serious trouble. Apart from causing death or injuries, getting wet unnecessarily can result in hypothermia (see pp154–55). After any river crossing, try to get group members as warm and dry as possible and be alert for symptoms of hypothermia.

It is often wisest to wait it out if the river seems to be flowing quickly but is likely to subside, or to look for an alternative route. If there is no option, then plan your crossing carefully. Spend some time moving up and down the bank, studying the river and its flow patterns, and then choose the best crossing point. If you have a sturdy rope then the crossing can be made much more safely.

ROPE-ASSISTED CROSSINGS

When using ropes to cross a river, the safest method is a continuous loop.
This is only suitable when at least three or more people are crossing.

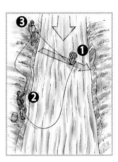

- Person 1 (the strongest) secures rope around chest to become part of the loop. Persons 2 and 3, downstream and upstream respectively, are not tied to the loop but feed rope out as person 1 crosses the river.
- Person 1 reaches the bank and unties himself. Person 2 secures himself to loop before walking to 3. He enters water and is belayed (rope held taut) by 3, while 1 keeps rope taut from opposite bank to guide 2 across.

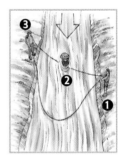

- Person 2 reaches person 1 on the bank, unties and walks downstream to take up loop. Person 3 secures himself and crosses, supported by person 1 who holds rope taut and bears most of rope weight, while 2 belays.

If a large group needs to cross a river, the continuous rope loop can be kept running until the last member is safely across. A safety line can also be tied across the river and the group can cross holding on to it while being belayed by another rope. Bear in mind that the tensioned line should preferably be angled downstream. This makes crossing the river easier because one struggles less against the flow of the water.

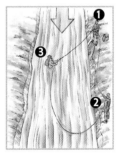

TIPS ON ROPELESS RIVER CROSSINGS

- Choose a crossing spot with no visible hazards immediately below it and don't cross just above cataracts and waterfalls.
- Cross diagonally with the current rather than trying to fight it. Always face upstream during crossings so that you can see ahead and therefore avoid any debris sweeping towards you.
- If possible, avoid crossing on river bends since water always flows fastest on the outside of bends.
- Take note that rocks and submerged obstacles often cause surface waves. Large boulders in fast-moving water can form dangerous 'eddies' (when a current reverses behind an obstacle) and whirlpools in the river below them.
- Sticks or poles can be used to provide mutual support or hold a group together. If the current is strong, hold the sticks firmly with arms crossed at chest level.
- Crossing in a group line with a sturdy pole for support also gives support to smaller, weaker or less sure-footed individuals. The simplest method is to form a line with the strongest person upstream to break the flow of current.
- Another method is to form a group 'huddle' by all facing inwards, linking arms across each other's shoulders and then crossing the river by shuffling sideways. The person on the leading side of the huddle could use a stick for balance as well as to assess the depth and obstacle risk on the riverbed.
- For an individual crossing or wading across wide shallow streams that flow slowly, it is best to use a pole or stick both for support and to test the depth ahead. Hold the pole firmly with both hands.
- If crossing with a heavy backpack, loosen the hip belt of the pack. If you lose your balance you can easily remove the backpack to avoid being swept along face-down underneath it.
- Flotation aids can be made from a waterproofed pack, airfilled long trousers (see p12) or even empty water bottles. A tent flysheet stuffed with grass or light but bulky substances (e.g. polystyrene, empty plastic bottles and foam mattresses) may also help with flotation.

Makeshift bridges

One of the easiest and safest ways of crossing a deep gorge or a narrow, fast-flowing stream is to build a bridge. This is particularly useful if you need to cross a stream regularly, either in a long-term survival situation of a few days or more, or if you need to regularly cross streams around a base camp.

SIMPLE LOG BRIDGE

The advantage of a log bridge for narrow streams and ravines is that it can initially be built entirely from one side of a river.

(a) Secure a short log at cross-angles to the intended bridge on the bank edge, using stakes to fix it in place.
(b) Brace a log against the short one.

(c) Use rope to raise the bridging log along the bank and over river.
(d) Swing it across and drop the end on the opposite bank.

(e) Slide a second, then a third log along the first one.
(f) Manoeuvre them until three or four logs bridge the stream. Use wooden or metal stakes to peg the logs firmly on both sides.

MONKEY BRIDGE

To create this bridge you will need a person or team on both sides of the gap.

- Each must create, for each end of the bridge, a simple, well-anchored X-frame around 2m (6$^1/_2$ ft) high and thoroughly shear-lashed (see p59) in the centre.
- Lash a crosspiece low across the legs of each X-frame, dig the legs firmly into the ground, push the X-frame up to about 45 degrees and anchor the crosspiece of each X-frame to sturdy stakes or trees.
- Span your thickest rope(s) from a solid anchor a few metres back from the X-frame over the middle of each X. This serves as the walking rope.
- Place some sacking or material under the rope on the X of the frame to prevent it wearing through as it moves under the weight of the group.
- Then push both X-frames upright to tension the rope. Attach your handrail ropes to the upper arms of each X and tension them back to suitable anchors.
- Adjust the tension of the bridge by pulling on the ropes anchoring the X-frames. The bridge can be made more stable if you place tensioned ropes out at roughly a 45° angle back from the top of each arm of the X-frames.

Bamboo poles lashed tightly to-gether serve as an effective walking surface in this monkey bridge.

In this instance, side ropes help to improve the stability of a longer swing bridge.

SMALL CRAFT SAFETY

- If possible, every person should have a life jacket or some good flotation aid.
- Flotation aids can be made from empty plastic bottles or tins, expanded polystyrene foam, inner tubes or waterproof material tied into a sausage (filling it with grass or similar light packing helps to retain its shape).
- Rolled-up foam mattresses, chunks of wood or empty bottles can also be used as flotation aids. If ditched in turbulent water, look around for anything, however small, that will help keep you afloat.
- Do not overload boats – righting or bailing a craft in midstream can be almost impossible and endanger crew members.
- Keep people in the craft positioned as low as possible to aid stability.

Sea anchors

Sea anchors, used to keep the nose of a craft into the wind and waves, are very valuable in high seas and heavy winds. In addition, they reduce drift, making it easier for searchers to locate your craft. In fast-flowing rivers, a sea anchor reduces speed and helps to maintain direction. It can be made from a bucket, an old tube or any piece of tough material sewn into a funnel shape. Even a log can be used if you have nothing else available.

A log tied to the back of a boat makes an effective sea anchor.

FLOTATION AND BOAT SAFETY

A raft is useful as it can be used to ferry small children, aged or injured members as well as supplies across a wide, slow river.

Rafts can be made from logs or from thick bamboo. If timber is wet it may cause your raft to float partially submerged – however, it is still possible to use such a raft. In planning the building of a raft, take into account the intended load and make your craft large enough to cope with it.

RAFT BUILDING

1. Begin with a base of two long poles lying across a shorter pole.
2. Cut a notch along the length of two logs, to act as retaining logs.
3. Place these, notch face-up, at right angles at either end of the raft base.
4. Arrange the rest of the logs to lie firmly within the notches.
5. Carve a notch along the length of two final logs, and secure them crosswise at each end of the raft, lashing tightly to hold the raft together.

Oars can be made from a flat piece of wood or several equal lengths of bamboo lashed together, then tied onto a long branch. A small X-frame lashed to the back of the raft can act as a support for the oar or rudder.

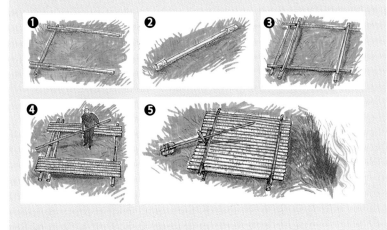

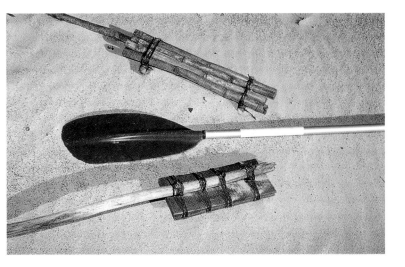

These makeshift oars can be as effective in the water as the commercially produced oar seen here. Make all lashings as tight as possible.

Putting the pieces together

- **Oars:** These can double as rudders. If there are no large, flat pieces of wood available, you can make a broader rudder by lashing numerous small pieces together. (The rudder can be fastened to the rear of the raft by means of a small X-frame lashed to the back spars.)

- **Sails:** If you are in a situation where you need to create sailing craft, constructing the sail so that you are able to angle it as well as raise and lower it lets you take advantage of differing wind directions. Two small sails (one on each side) add versatility and mean you can use smaller pieces of material. Even big towels can form useful sails. The mast and support beams can be anchored to the base via small logs set in a square.

- **Dugout canoes:** It is very difficult to make a dugout canoe from a tree trunk, but if you have the tools, sufficient time and large soft logs, then this could be a good option for crossing rivers, lakes or even the sea. Stability in a dugout is achieved by making the base broader and thicker and the sides relatively thin. A tapered, elevated nose ensures that it moves easily through the water.

IN THE MOUNTAINS

- Descent is more difficult than ascent because you cannot pick out good spots for your feet when coming down a slope.
- If you have to cross steep, snow-covered slopes and don't have a rope or climbing gear, send the strongest member (leader) ahead, preferably with a sharpened stick for support.
- The leader should trample out a ledge for others to follow.

In the 'short roping' technique, a stronger member holds someone on a tight rein – by varying the slack slightly, he gives the less sure-footed member valuable support on steep, broken ground.

- When walking across a slope, don't lean far into it – you'll be off balance and your feet could easily slip.
- Try to walk 'on balance' – as straight up as possible.
- Descending a steep slope is best done in a gradual zigzag pattern by kicking holes or steps and standing in them with your heels.
- When turning corners, it is very useful to have a sturdy pole or stick for added support.
- If the slope gets very steep, it is easier to descend backwards, facing the slope, kicking your toes in and digging your hands in as you go. If you do not have gloves, use a pair of socks on your hands to prevent frostbite (see p156).

Using ropes and harnesses

A rope is of limited value without proper training and a good set of equipment. Overconfidence or over-reliance on ropes can cause accidents. It is best to practise the elements of rope usage which focus on the emergency use of ropes. If possible, attend a registered climbing course offered by a reputable climbing instructor or training school before you embark on a trip to a steep mountain area. Modern alpine climbers seldom make use of only a rope – their climbing equipment also includes harnesses, carabiners, slings and protection gear.

Anchoring the rope and belayer

A rope can only provide security if it is properly anchored and 'belayed'. It can then be used safely to help people up steep sections or to lower them down others. Note that anchor points must be solid and tied off with a figure-of-eight knot (see pp57–58).

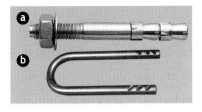

A: a sleeve anchor expansion bolt is strong and durable. B: a glue-in staple with knurled ends can hold a large load.

- The belayer is tied on to the anchor and holds the rope around his waist, controlling any fall by the friction of pulling it tightly around his body.
- The anchor, the belayer and the rope to the climber should lie in as straight a line as possible.

A traditional (classic) abseil needs practice as well as suitable clothing to avoid rope burns to the neck and groin area.

- When climbing, firmly hold the belay rope and never let go for even a fraction of a second.
- During a mountain descent, the last person can slide down the rope if he/she knows how to do so. This climbing technique, known as 'abseiling' (rappelling) allows for the last person to come down a doubled rope. If the rope is placed correctly, you will be able to pull it down for later use.
- As the lower hand controls the speed by creating friction around the body, do not try to support yourself with your upper hand. Also, remember to pad the neck area to prevent rope burns on your neck.
- Abseiling is a dangerous technique, especially when you only use a rope and you have not had sufficient practice. This technique is suitable for mildly angled descents and should not ever be attempted on vertical or overhanging rock.

Improvised harnesses

A climbing harness tied around the waist is useful, especially for children, elderly or injured climbers.

A modified harness can be made from slings, webbing, safety belts or from other pieces of rope. The harness should be strong and be arranged to ensure that the point of attachment is higher than the person's waist.

A 'safety rail' – made simply by tying knots or loops at intervals in a rope – can be very helpful for novice climbers to grab onto. The rope rail can even be used as handy footholds or 'steps' when climbing up or down steeper slopes.

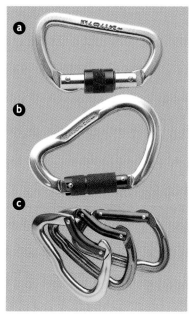

a: a screwgate locks this carabiner.
b: this carabiner gate is auto-locking.
c: clipgates can be straight or bent.

When used for belaying, anchors should be able to take strain in any direction – up, down or sideways.
Inset: A friction hitch knot.

Carabiners

If you have a screwgate carabiner (the metal snaplinks used to connect ropes and other climbing gear), then you can belay safely using a friction hitch knot. This knot allows you to take in slack without your body needing to be part of the belay. When reversed through the carabiner, the same knot can also be used for lowering people or objects that are tied to the rope.

TRAVELLING ON GLACIERS AND AVALANCHES

If there is any chance that a glacier has hidden crevasses (deep holes covered by light snow or snow bridges), then a group should be roped together 6–10m (20–30ft) apart with the rope kept fairly taut. The leader goes ahead, testing the snow with ski poles or an ice axe. Should anyone fall into a crevasse, the other members should fall down, dig in their heels, and try to brake his fall. Use whatever techniques you can to haul the person out of the crevasse as soon as possible. Reduce friction on the rope by padding the rope where it cuts into the crevasse.

Avalanches leave little time for preparation; running out of their path is the best initial action.

It is not advisable to travel across steeply sloping ice fields without using crampons (toothed spikes that fasten on a climber's boots) and an ice axe unless you have considerable experience.

Avalanche survival

- If you get caught in an avalanche, try to move to the surface or the side by making vigorous 'swimming' movements with your hands and feet.
- When the avalanche starts to slow down, pummel the snow around you with your hands, legs and arms to create an air space. Lie still – if you can see light, you might be near the surface.
- Listen for sounds of rescue and shout ONLY when rescuers are very close.
- If no rescue arrives within a few minutes, then dig upward.
- Letting saliva dribble out of your mouth will help you find up and down direction.
- Rest frequently and continue listening for voices or sounds of a rescue team.
- If you see someone else caught in an avalanche, try to keep watching them as long as possible.
- When the avalanche stops, move to the point where they were last seen and then search rapidly downhill.
- Shout at intervals and listen in total silence for any faint reply. If you have long thin sticks, use them to prod in the snow for the victim(s).

JUNGLE TRAVEL

There are seldom landmarks in the jungle and it is easy to become dis-orientated. A compass is an invaluable tool; refer to it often. If not available, try to get sightings through other methods.

- Try to get sightings on the sun or stars to maintain your direction.
- Alternatively, spread your group members out as far as possible with-out losing contact and keep your line of travel by moving according to the Triplet method (see p123).
- Cut plants low down on both sides of the path to avoid leaving stems for others to trip on.
- Sever spikes of vegetation completely – especially bamboo – as this can be dangerous if someone falls onto them.

To avoid disorientation in dense jungles or bush, make frequent use of a compass. Getting to an elevated area safely (e.g. up a tree or cliff) makes it easier to scout for landmarks or signs of civilization.

- Change the lead person often to prevent exhaustion.
- Even though humidity and rainfall levels are high in the jungle, mov-ing around may still cause you to become severely dehydrated.
- Be careful of cliffs or steep drops.
- Loose, damp vegetation underfoot is also hazardous as you can easily slip down a steep slope.
- Check constantly for leeches and other parasites.
- Never pull a leech off as this can leave a nasty scar that festers easily. Rather dab it with a burning ciga-rette or stick – the leech will fall off with little or no real damage. Turpentine or petrol can also be used to rid your body of leeches.

A machete or 'panga' is the most effective tool for cutting through dense tropical bush. Take care not to blunt the machete on rocks or to injure others when using it.

UNDERSTANDING WEATHER

Large-scale weather changes can often be gauged by the appearance of high clouds (e.g. cirrus or altostratus). These high cloud formations predict the passage of a warm front that precedes a major cold front by a few hours. True storm clouds – called cumulonimbus 'thunderheads' – will warn that bad weather is close at hand.

Other features in nature that indicate bad weather include:

- Dramatic changes in wind speeds and patterns.
- Unusual and frantic animal activity as well as a diminishing ring around the moon (corona).
- Changes in barometric pressure – provided you have a barometer. This is the most reliable indicator.

- A drop in air pressure (indicated on an altimeter as a 'rise' in altitude even though you are still remaining in one place) is a sure sign of impending bad weather. Likewise, a rise in pressure (i.e. a 'drop' in altitude) indicates an improvement in weather conditions.

Wind speeds in cyclones can easily lift you off your feet. Seek cover.

A hiker caught in a flash flood uses vegetation to support himself in the torrent.

MEDICAL
KNOW-HOW

Whether you are on a gentle hike in the country or days from civilization on a multi-day mountain trek, once you have lost access to conventional emergency medical services, it's up to you to effectively manage any medical situation that may occur. This could be anything from a minor condition to a full-blown, life-threatening medical emergency. A rapid assessment of the situation needs to be made, the accident scene made as safe as possible – the group's safety is of primary importance – and urgent medical attention provided.

Consider what the likely hazards are before embarking on a journey. People suffering from medical conditions such as heart disease, diabetes, asthma, epilepsy, etc. require special consideration when visiting remote areas that lack medical facilities.

Because rescue operations demand a lot of time, energy, and specialized skills, you should make every effort to avoid getting into such a scenario.

HAZARD

Protect yourself, others and the patient from further harm.
- If, for example, you are on steep ground, first secure the patient and rescuer with a rope if possible and assess the danger of loose falling rocks.
- Only in an extremely hazardous situation, such as a fire, should the patient be moved without first carrying out a proper medical assessment.
- If available, don latex gloves before touching body fluids although the major risks – HIV and Hepatitis B virus – cannot penetrate intact skin.
- Scrupulously safeguard any sharp objects that are contaminated with blood (glass shards, injection needles).

HELLO

Talk to the patient.
- Is the patient conscious? Do you have permission to treat?
- If the patient answers back you know that the brain is functioning and immediate cardiopulmonary resuscitation (CPR) is unnecessary.
- Immediate verbal reassurance is important.

HELP

Access emergency services.
- Call people around you to come and help if they are not yet aware of the emergency.
- Decide whether to call for outside help before starting emergency treatment. In a wilderness setting it may take hours for help to arrive.

ABC PRINCIPLES

Airway, Breathing, Circulation.
The rescuer should perform a primary survey to check for life-threatening conditions that require immediate attention. Using the ABC approach helps the rescuer focus on the most critical determinants of survival in the first few minutes after an accident.

- **Airway**
Ensure the airway is open.
- **Breathing**
If not breathing, give artificial ventilation.
- **Circulation**
Stop any bleeding. If the heart has stopped, perform heart massage.

Plans of action

Once you have the situation under control, life-saving measures have been applied and help is on the way, you can continue treating the patient. The main treatment principles are: avoid doing further harm, relieve pain and cover wounds to prevent any infection. Keep talking to the patient while you are busy with treatment.

Medical evacuation

Getting expert medical assistance to the patient fast is a better option than trying to transport an unstable patient in a makeshift fashion. Once a paramedic is on the scene, he/she can stabilize the patient by placing a tube in the

A casualty with a serious head injury is made comfortable before being assessed according to the AVPU system.

windpipe to secure the airway, administering intravenous fluid to counteract shock and giving oxygen as well as powerful painkillers prior to transport.

Waiting for help to arrive

- Patients must be actively nursed and looked after. They should never be left alone unless this is unavoidable.
- Try to make patients as comfortable as possible and place suitable padding and insulation between them and the ground.
- Construct a sun/wind/rain shelter and keep them warm.
- Conscious patients can be given fluids, preferably containing a little sugar, in small quantities at a time unless they are expected to be in hospital within four hours. In this case it is better to give them nothing at all in case they require surgery.
- Help them with going to the toilet. If they are able to pass some urine about every four hours (adults), you can be assured that they are not dehydrated or in circulation failure.
- Continue to monitor their vital signs in case there is deterioration.
- Continually encourage and reassure the patient. Let him/her sleep if he/she wants to – there is no point in trying to keep a patient awake who appears to be lapsing into a coma.

Evacuating the patient on foot

- Do not underestimate the formidable task of carrying someone on a stretcher for any appreciable distance.
- Mountain rescue stretchers are designed so that up to 10 carriers can share the load and even then, carriers have to be rotated approximately every 30 minutes.
- Makeshift stretchers or sledges are two options for carrying a patient. However, neither method is suitable if the patient has a spinal injury.
- A more viable option is to try to walk the patient out. This is obviously not possible if the patient is severely injured and shocked, has a decreased level of consciousness, has breathing problems or has suspected neck, back or pelvic injuries.
- If you can safely stand the patient up with two supporting persons, one on each side, and a lot of encouragement, it is amazing what progress can be made.

Walking the patient out may be an option if injuries are minor.

INFORMATION THAT MAY BE REQUIRED BY RESCUE TEAM

- Nature of incident (e.g. injury, illness).
- Cause of injury (e.g. fall).
- Exact location (use more than one description):
  GPS position
  map coordinates
  distance and direction from identifiable feature
  description of topography.
- Number of patients.
- Name and age of each patient.
- Medical condition of patients:
  vital signs
  injuries
  treatment applied.
- Local weather conditions.
- Local access difficulties (e.g. patient is on a cliff face).
- Site of helicopter landing zone.
- Number of uninjured members of the group.

- Group equipment:
  shelter
  food
  medical supplies.
- Signalling methods.
- Medical expertise in group.

BLOCKAGES OF THE AIRWAY

The most valuable first aid a bystander can do for a patient is to ensure that the airway through which he/she breathes stays open. If the airway blocks, we die in minutes. The airway consists of the mouth or nose, back of the throat, voice box and windpipe. While awake or asleep, we are accustomed to being able to do routine actions that keep our airways open – swallowing, coughing and opening the mouth.

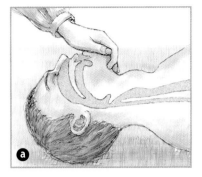

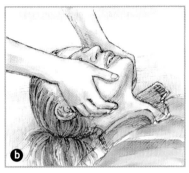

In a conscious patient, airway blockage can result from severe facial injuries, insect bites, swelling from infection, inhalation of hot gases or a solid piece of food that 'goes the wrong way' and then gets stuck in the voice box.

If the airway is completely blocked, the patient will breathe with difficulty for a few minutes and then stop as the brain becomes depressed due to lack of oxygen. When the airway is partly blocked, the patient will struggle to breathe in and snore, gurgle or make a high pitched sound; there may be recessing (sucking in) of the ribcage and throat.

In an unconscious patient, the airway protection reflexes can lower. Without these reflexes, an unconscious person lying on his back will tend to block his airway because the back of the tongue falls against the back of the throat. There is also a risk of inhaling blood or vomit present in the mouth.

An unconscious patient should be placed onto his side in the recovery position to prevent inhalation of blood or vomit.

- Open the airway by pushing the lower jawbone forward (see chin lift illustration [a]) or use the jaw-thrust manoeuvre (applying pressure behind both angles of the jaw [b]).
- At the same time, hold the neck in a neutral position in case there is an associated neck fracture.
- You may have to put your finger in the mouth to remove any obstruction (e.g. lumps of food or false teeth) that is blocking the upper part of the airway.

Recovery Position

- Unconscious patients should always be turned onto their side in the 'recovery position' (see right), with the head resting on the left forearm, bent at the elbow.
- Remember to protect the neck and spine while moving an injured patient into this position.
- Keep the patient in the recovery position even during transport – it ensures that gravity keeps the airway open.
- If necessary, make a makeshift suction pump out of a plastic bottle and a plastic tube.

Heimlich manoeuvre

If a patient gets a solid piece of food stuck in the voice box, he/she is unable to talk; however, he/she should be able to signal any distress by making a choking sign at the throat.

In adults

- Stand behind the patient (who should be standing or sitting) and wrap your arms around his/her chest.
- Make a fist and cover it with your other hand, then press hard and rapidly upwards in the centre of the abdomen, just below the ribcage, while compressing the ribcage with your arms (see illustration left).
- Repeat this action until the obstruction has been dislodged.
- If the victim loses consciousness first, check in the mouth for any foreign object, which should be removed; then start the CPR sequence.

Small children

- First check the mouth for removable objects.
- Hold face down and thump between the shoulder blades to dislodge the obstruction.

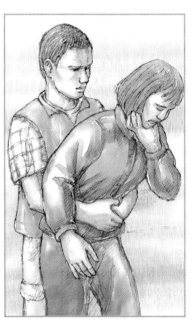

BREATHING

Having established that the airway is open, the next most important thing is to see if the patient is breathing. Breathing is controlled by the brain – if the heart stops and the brain receives no oxygen, breathing will also stop.

Some breathing problems are caused by injuries to the chest, accumulation of fluid in the lungs caused by altitude and after a near-drowning incident, pneumo-

nia or an acute asthma attack. The normal resting breath rate for an adult is 15 to 25 breaths per minute. More than 30 breaths per minute may be an indication of a breathing problem.

Always assume that breathing difficulties are serious and get help promptly. Let the patient sit up if he/she is more comfortable that way. Give oxygen if you have an available supply.

Without professional medical help, some survivors have to use common sense and apply first-aid principles.

Cardiopulmonary Resuscitation

Cardiopulmonary resuscitation (CPR) is best learnt on a training course but the following is a brief guideline.

Resuscitation efforts should be performed promptly and proficiently, but it should be recognized that CPR offers a slight chance of survival to a patient with cardiac arrest.

In cardiac arrests resulting from injury (especially head injuries or bleeding), survival is unlikely unless the arrest is caused by short-term airway obstruction. Situations where CPR may save a life are cardiac arrest from hypothermia, near-drowning and lightning strike.

Steps to follow:
- Place the patient on his back.
- Kneel at his side and place the heel of your hand in the centre of the lower half of his chest, with your other hand resting on the first.
- Thrust down with straight arms, depressing the chest by 4–5cm (2in).
- Pause after 15 compressions, and give two breaths (over two seconds each) of mouth-to-mouth respiration.
- Do 100 compressions per minute.
- After four cycles, check for breathing and a pulse.

Standard guidelines recommend that unless the pulse returns, CPR must be continued until professional help arrives or until the rescuers are exhausted. If you are out in the wilderness and medical help is hours away, you will have to decide yourself when to stop. Survival after 15 minutes of CPR is very unlikely, except in the case of hypothermia.

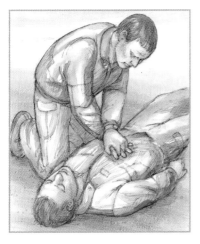

SPINAL IMMOBILIZATION

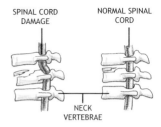

If the patient has been injured, particularly as a result of a fall or traffic accident, assume that a spinal (neck or back) injury has occurred and take steps to ensure that the neck and spine are stabilized. This means that the patient should lie still and the neck should be kept in a neutral position – not twisted, bent forwards, backwards or sideways. Any movement of the patient should only occur after you have confidently excluded a neck or spinal injury, or after you have immobilized the neck with a rigid collar and the spine on a stiff board or stretcher. The only exception is if it is essential to move the patient to avoid immediate, life-threatening external danger. Assume that all

Movement of an unstable neck or back fracture can further damage the patient's spinal cord.

unconscious, injured patients have a spinal injury until ruled out by an X-ray. Conscious patients who have no pain in the neck or spine and no numbness or paralysis of the limbs probably do not have a spinal injury.

This injured girl has been placed between some tightly packed items to prevent any movement and to keep her neck and spine immobile until help arrives.

BLEEDING

After opening the airway and CPR, the next most important priority is to stop any bleeding.

Stop arterial bleeding by applying direct pressure on the wound and using a bandage to maintain the pressure.

- Locate the source of the bleeding.
- Control bleeding by applying firm direct pressure on the bleeding site using a clean piece of cloth (preferably sterile wound dressing), or your hand (or the patient's hand).
- To stop arterial bleeding, press hard to apply direct pressure on the dressing for at least three minutes, then maintain the pressure with a bandage.
- If the dressing and bandage become soaked with blood, apply a second dressing over the first one.
- Elevate the bleeding point and check that there are no constrictions around the limb above the bleeding point (e.g. a rolled-up trouser leg), which will encourage venous bleeding.
- Pressure points are no longer recommended to control bleeding. Only use tourniquets as a last resort to stop bleeding after a traumatic amputation e.g. loss of a limb from a shark attack.

The body will try to conserve blood flow to vital organs by reducing the circulation to the skin and limbs. The patient will look pale, anxious and sweaty; breathing and pulse will be fast. Other signs of shock are cold hands and feet, and it will be difficult to feel the patient's pulse at the wrist. In advanced shock, the patient becomes confused and loses consciousness.

Treatment for shock

- Stop further bleeding, and keep the patient still while lying flat.
- Elevate the legs – this returns some blood to the central circulation. Do not move a shocked patient.
- It is unlikely that the intravenous fluid solution used by medical rescuers to replace the blood lost will be available to you; it requires skill to administer.
- Internal bleeding can occur from penetrating or blunt injuries to the chest and abdomen. There is no way of controlling this type of bleeding except with surgery. Treat for shock as above and hope the bleeding stops.

Brain injuries

Injuries to the brain are indicated by some disturbance in consciousness

Fractures should be splinted to reduce pain and prevent further tissue damage.

including extreme restlessness. Any period of unconsciousness should be regarded as very serious. One danger is that bleeding inside the skull may compress the brain, causing a deepening level of unconsciousness. The only treatment for this condition is urgent neurosurgery. Bear in mind that maintaining an open airway is the most important thing you can do for someone with a brain injury.

Fractures

The symptoms of a fracture – intense pain, inability to move the limb and deformity – are usually obvious and can be seen more readily by comparing it with the normal limb. Multiple fractures or those involving the femur (thighbone) can cause enough blood loss to result in shock and death. Open fractures (where a wound overlies the fracture) require urgent surgery to clean out the wound and prevent infection. Fractures with damaged nerves and arteries are also more serious. Check for movement of the toes or fingers and for the presence of a pulse below the fracture site.

Fractures must be splinted to reduce pain and to prevent further tissue injury and blood loss from movement. You can splint a leg to the opposite leg and the arm to the chest. Any suitable straight, rigid object such as an ice axe or branch can be adapted as a splint.

MEDICAL KNOW-HOW

A makeshift leg splint can be made by using a closed-cell foam mattress and climbing slings.

Chest injuries

The most common chest injury is broken ribs. This is very painful and causes breathing problems. It is difficult for the patient to cough and clear secretions and this can result in pneumonia. A collection of air or blood between the lung and the chest wall can complicate rib fractures and also cause breathing difficulties. This is treated by a doctor or paramedic inserting a thick tube with a one-way valve between the ribs to drain the blood or air.

Treat rib fractures by giving pain-relieving medication and allowing the patient to sit up.

Wounds

Non-bleeding wounds:

- Gently clean with a sterile dressing.
- Remove any debris without precipitating further bleeding.
- Cover the wound with a sterile dressing.
- Leave firmly embedded objects for later removal in hospital.

- Clean-cut wound edges can be held together with adhesive strips.
- Patients with wounds should get a tetanus vaccine booster if they have not had one in the past three years.

Burns

- Immediately remove the patient from burning material.
- Cool the burned area by immersing it in clean water or pouring water on it.
- Cover the burn with a sterile dressing or a clean cloth.
- Do not try to clean the burn and do not apply ointments.
- Full thickness burns with skin destruction will need skin grafting later.
- Large burns (more than 20 per cent of the body surface area) can cause enough plasma loss to result in shock.
- Urgent hospitalization is required for large burns and other burns on the face and hands.

Sprains

These are injuries to the soft tissues surrounding joints where the muscles, ligaments and tendons are stretched or torn.

- To treat a sprain, adhere to the RICE principle – Rest, Ice, Compression and Elevation. Stop walking, rest and apply ice, snow, or cold water – if available.
- Strap the sprained ankle with broad, non-stretchable tape to hold it in the opposite way to the direction of injury.

Steady traction using a weight on the arm (in this survival situation, helpers have weighted a helmet by placing a rock inside it) with the patient lying in this position is the safest way of reducing a dislocated shoulder. As it requires skill to correct or reduce a dislocation, it is best to learn the correct technique by attending a good first-aid course.

- Apply the tape from the top of the foot, around the inside of the foot, under the instep, then up the outer side of the ankle and lower leg.
- Apply a firm, elastic bandage over the tape to further support the limb.
- Elevate the limb to help reduce swelling; administer an anti-inflammatory tablet to lessen the pain.
- If it is essential to continue walking, do not remove the boot after an ankle sprain, as swelling may prevent you getting the boot back on.
- Once the initial swelling and pain have subsided, the sprained joint should be mildly and progressively exercised.

Dislocations

Dislocations are serious joint injuries that cause bone displacement. They are very painful and the affected limb cannot be used. In hip and shoulder dislocations, the long bone literally comes out of the joint socket. The limb's nerve and blood supply may be affected and require urgent medical attention.

Dislocations can often be reduced or corrected by firmly pulling the limb while pushing the bone back into the joint, immediately after an injury. This also helps to ease the pain.

This is not an easy process, and fractures can occur or worsen, but in a survival situation it is worth attempting it. In other cases, splint a dislocated limb as you would for a fracture (see p150).

ENVIRONMENTAL EMERGENCIES

Heat-related illness

Minor heat-related conditions include heat rash, heat edema (feet swelling), heat cramps and heat syncope. The latter is a faint that occurs after stopping vigorous exercise in a hot environment and is caused by a period of low blood pressure from excessive dilation of the blood vessels. Treat by lying in the shade and rehydrating with increased fluid intake.

Heat exhaustion

This is the most common of the more serious heat-related conditions. Symptoms include exhaustion, dizziness, mild mental changes, nausea and headache. The patient may pant and sweat profusely. Treat by resting in the shade, rehydrating and removing excess clothing. Avoid any anti-inflammatory drugs such as aspirin or Ibuprofen as they could increase the risk of kidney failure.

Heat stroke

This rare but serious condition can be fatal. The body temperature can rise as high as 46°C/115°F (normal 37°C/98.6°F) but the main symptoms of heat stroke are confusion, seizures and coma. Some patients may not sweat despite the heat, although others sweat profusely.

Treat by fanning and aggressive cooling with water. Keep the patient in the recovery position, watch the airway and arrange for urgent hospitalization.

In hot desert terrain it is important to conserve body moisture. Shelter from the burning sun under a makeshift tent weighted with stones to prevent serious conditions such as heat exhaustion and heat stroke.

COLD-RELATED CONDITIONS
Hypothermia
Hypothermia occurs when the body fails to conserve heat, causing uncontrollable shivering and mental confusion. Unless the heat loss is prevented, the patient's condition will deteriorate, resulting in coma, cardiac arrest and death.

Hypothermia occurs most often with immersion in cold water and hiking in wet, cold and windy conditions. It is aggravated by hunger, fatigue, illness and high altitude.

Prevention
- Wetsuits and flotation devices should be worn by small-craft occupants at risk of prolonged immersion in cold water. Immersion victims lose the ability to swim before they lose consciousness.
- Hikers should carry synthetic, fibre-pile jackets, trousers and headgear as well as outer garments that are wind-proof and water-protected.

Body temperature drops rapidly in cold water, causing muscle weakness and an inability to help oneself.

- Carry some emergency shelter – a tent or a large plastic bivvie-bag.
- Don't pressurize unfit companions to continue with long exhausting hikes in bad weather.
- Ensure that all group members frequently snack on high-energy food such as chocolate.

Treatment
- Get the victim into dry clothes, then place in a sleeping bag inside a tent that is insulated from the ground.
- If dry clothes are not available, use a plastic covering to prevent heat loss by evaporation.
- Cover the head as it loses heat more rapidly than other parts of the body.
- The body heat of companions can warm a patient.
- Avoid hot objects applied to the skin as they can easily cause burning because of the reduced blood supply to the skin.
- Conscious patients should be given plenty of warm liquids to replace high urine loss.
- If the patient is unconscious place him/her in the recovery position and monitor the airway constantly.
- Give mouth to mouth respiration if breathing ceases; administer CPR if the heart stops. Severe hypothermia mimics brain death, and when in doubt, continue with CPR until the patient has been warmed up.

STAGES OF HYPOTHERMIA

Mild

Core temperature 35°C–32°C
(95°F–92°F)

- Complains of severe cold
- Poor judgement, confusion, irritability
- Slurred speech, stumbling
- Uncontrollable shivering
- Cold, blue hands and feet
- Stiff muscles
- High urine production leading to dehydration

Moderate

Core temperature 32°C–28°C
(90°F–82.4°F)

- Decreased level of consciousness
- Shivering may stop
- Muscles are stiff and rigid
- Irregular heartbeat

Severe

Core temperature below
28°C (82.2°F)

- Deeply unconscious
- Slow breathing
- Slow, irregular heartbeat
- Heart may stop

Passive re-warming after being swept into a river is adequate for someone with mild or moderate hypothermia. Use any means to prevent heat loss.

A polythene exposure bag (left) is more effective than a metallic exposure blanket (right). Get out of the wind and prevent heat loss from the head.

Frostbite

This condition occurs when tissue freezes and most commonly affects the fingers, nose, ears and toes. Frostbite may cause permanent tissue damage, leading to gangrene and amputation. General hypothermia and dehydration precipitate the condition by reducing the body's blood supply to peripheral areas. Constrictive clothing, tight boots and smoking can be aggravating factors.

Prevention

- Stay warm and keep affected parts as warm as possible.
- Always carry an extra pair of mittens in subzero conditions.
- Re-warm a patient with early frostbite immediately, except if the affected limbs have to be used to get to safety.
- Re-freezing a limb after thawing is worse than keeping it frozen. It is essential to minimize tissue damage in frostbitten tissue.

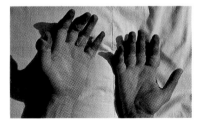

Severe frostbite can lead to gangrene, requiring amputation, so prevention is better than cure.

- Do not rub affected parts and try to keep all weight and pressure off the limbs, particularly once they have started to thaw – rapid thawing is far better than slow thawing.
- Once the patient is at a place where he can be kept warm, immerse the affected part in warm water. Maintain it at a 40°C (104°F) temperature; don't let it exceed 44°C (111°F).

This hiker's 'sunglasses', made from dark negative film, act as improvised eye protection to prevent snow blindness.

Snow blindness

UV entering the eye damages the cornea, causing inflammation and pain. Symptoms often do not show up for 10–12 hours after exposure. In snow conditions, wear sunglasses with side shields or wraparound lenses. Emergency glasses can be made by cutting slits in cardboard or by using a strip of dark negative film.

ALTITUDE MOUNTAIN SICKNESS (AMS)

Acute AMS usually only occurs above 2000m (6000ft). Symptoms are headache, loss of appetite, nausea, insomnia, dizziness, decreased urine output and swollen feet. These symptoms will only appear 12–24 hours after reaching high altitude and are caused by a decreased oxygen supply to the brain. Dehydration from hyperventilating dry air also plays a part. Two serious complications of AMS, namely high altitude pulmonary edema (HAPE) and high altitude cerebral edema (HACE) occur in susceptible people. HAPE patients struggle to breathe and the lips appear blue. In advanced cases, the chest sounds as if it is full of bubbles and the patient may cough up foam. HACE causes intense headache and a decreasing level of consciousness.

A Sherpa mountain guide uses an adapted rope coil method for carrying an altitude sickness victim to lower elevation. The best treatment for HAPE and HACE is rapid descent.

Prevention

- Ascend slowly – preferably only 300m (1000ft) per day.
- The altitude at which one sleeps is more likely to cause AMS symptoms; therefore 'climb high, sleep low'.
- Arrange to spend a few days at 2500–3000m (8000–1000ft) before ascending further.
- Taking 125–250mg Acetazolamide (Diamox®) twice a day and starting 48 hours before reaching altitude will help to reduce symptoms.
- Drink enough liquid.

- Treat mild AMS by delaying further ascent and taking headache tablets e.g. Paracetamol (Acetaminophen).
- Avoid sleeping tablets and alcohol.
- Suspected HAPE or HACE is an emergency and immediate descent by 500–1000m (1500–3000ft) is essential. Administer oxygen if available.
- A Gamow bag is a portable, inflatable fabric bag in which a patient with AMS can be placed. The altitude is reduced by increasing the pressure in the bag with a foot bellows.

NEAR-DROWNING

Drowning is commonly associated with outdoor adventure activities, but is definitely preventable.

Prevention

- Insist that boaters wear life jackets.
- Ensure that children near water are always supervised.
- Do not combine alcohol intake with swimming.
- Only jump into the water to rescue a drowning victim if you are competent in lifesaving skills. Rather throw a rope or floatable object for the victim to cling to.

If the patient has stopped breathing:

- Start the ABC steps outlined on p141 immediately.
- Beware of a possible neck injury if the patient has just dived into the water.

An unconscious, breathing, near-drowning victim should be turned in the recovery position to prevent him sucking fluid into the airway (aspiration).

Do not attempt to rescue drowning victims if you lack lifesaving skills.

- If the patient is unconscious but breathing, place him/her in the recovery position – he/she is likely to vomit swallowed water – and keep the airway open.

Do CPR even after a long submersion as cold slightly prolongs the time the brain can function without oxygen. Submersion victims are at risk of developing 'secondary drowning' – breathing problems that develop later after inhaling water. Give patients oxygen and take to hospital.

BITES AND STINGS

Wearing suitable footwear, being very cautious where you put your hands and feet and inspecting your boots before putting them on can prevent bites from snakes and insects.

Snakebite

Our primordial fear of snakes makes snakebite one of the most overrated hazards of the outdoor experience. Most snakes have a simple philosophy – if you don't bother them, they won't bite you. The majority of snakebites occur while attempting to capture or play with these creatures. Snakebites are seldom fatal.

Snake toxin is designed to immobilize and help digest the prey. Neurotoxins produced mainly by the Elapidae group – the Cobras of Africa and Asia, the Mambas of Africa and Coral snakes of North America – cause muscle paralysis. Snakes that produce this poison are the most dangerous. Adders such as the Puff Adder found in Africa produce digesting toxins that are very painful and cause severe tissue damage around the bite. Less common toxins interfere with blood clotting and cause bleeding. Rattlesnakes are the most common cause of venomous bites in North America. Their toxin has mixed effects, causing both paralysis and tissue damage. Bites from this group of snakes only have a one per cent death rate.

You shouldn't:
- Try to catch the snake – the type of toxin involved will be indicated clearly by the symptoms.
- Cut the wound.
- Give any alcohol.
- Administer electric shocks.
- Apply a tourniquet; it will probably do more harm than good especially with a tissue toxin, although short-term use has saved victims from a neurotoxic bite.

You should:
- Calm the patient and avoid any movement which will spread the toxin.
- Apply a firm crepe dressing to the affected area and evacuate the patient by helicopter if possible.
- If there are signs of envenomation ('dry bites'), anti-snakebite serum can be effective.
- As a second option, suction the wound with a suction pump immediately.
- Watch for signs of respiratory depression and apply mouth-to-mouth resuscitation if necessary.

Bites from snakes can be prevented by wearing suitable footwear and long pants.

Spider and scorpion bites

Many spiders will inflict nasty bites but few are more than a nuisance. The exceptions are the potentially fatal bites by the Black Widow and Brown Widow of Europe, North America and Africa and the Funnel Web Spider of Australia. The Violin Spider of Africa can cause severe tissue damage – similar to a Puff Adder – but is seldom (if ever) fatal.

Treatment is much the same as for snakebite. Children with a smaller body mass are more at risk from the poisons produced by spiders.

Very few scorpions can cause death or serious harm to adults but, as with spiders, the sting is more dangerous to small children. A scorpion can sting multiple times and produce a toxin that affects the nervous system, causing writhing and jittery movements. A scorpion sting can be excruciatingly painful, and ice applied to the sting may help. Get medical help if any symptoms other than local pain develop.

The small pincers and large sting of this scorpion indicate a powerful sting.

Bee, wasp and hornet stings

Wasps, hornets and particularly bees are responsible for more deaths than snakes, spiders and scorpions combined (especially the African Honey Bee). A single bee sting is only a problem when a patient is hypersensitized to bees, perhaps because of previous stings or a natural allergy.

Antihistamine medication (injected or in tablet form) will help. Multiple bee stings can cause the victim to go into shock, cause respiratory depression and obstruction of the airway from swelling.

Anyone who has a natural allergy to bees should avoid contact with these insects.

After a severe attack:

- lie the victim down to prevent any movement
- remove the stings as soon as possible and apply CPR if needed
- fast removal is vital – bee stings continue to pump poison into the body for up to 20 minutes after an attack
- remove bee stings by scraping them off with a sharp blade or a needle
- never handle the sting – this causes more poison to enter the system.

Marine creatures

These can be divided into those that sting, such as jellyfish, bluebottles and fire coral, and those that 'stick' such as Stone Fish, Barbel and Scorpion Fish. Relieve the pain from 'stingers' by applying vinegar or alcohol to the sting. Pain from the 'stickers' may be quite intense and is relieved by submerging the affected part in water as hot as you can tolerate.

Boiling water is the surest way of decontaminating river water to be used for drinking purposes.

Scorpionfish use their spines in defense.

TRAVEL AND TROPICAL INFECTIONS

From a medical perspective, travelling in hot areas is more hazardous than in colder, more temperate zones. Higher temperatures allow bacteria to breed faster, promoting the growth of flies, ticks and other insects. To avoid many of these diseases, have the appropriate vaccinations and be careful in what you eat and drink. Always remember to tell your doctor where you have visited if you become ill after returning from a trip abroad.

Contaminated water and food

Most visitors to less-sophisticated countries are likely to experience travel-related diarrhoea (gastrointestinal disease).

Here's how to prevent travel-related infections:

- Use a water source that is as clean as possible.
- Eat hot, freshly prepared food or fruit that you peel yourself.
- Wash your hands often – especially before eating. People who have a fever or diarrhoea should not prepare food for others.
- Beware of ice made from contaminated water. Note that adding alcoholic beverages such as whisky does not make the ice safe.

Traveller's diarrhoea is caused by a variety of bacteria and viruses. It is usually a self-limiting infection that responds to rehydration with copious fluids.

- Add rehydration powder to fluids which replaces electrolyte loss.
- Alternatively, add one teaspoon of salt, with sugar to taste, to 1 litre (2pt) water.
- Medication that slows down bowel motion (e.g. Loperamide and Codeine) should be used with caution.
- More persistent diarrhoea with a fever usually responds to antibiotics such as Ciprofloxacin.

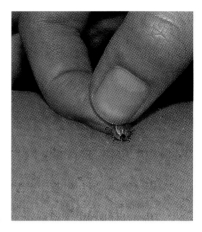

Remove ticks with care to prevent mouth parts remaining embedded in the skin.

Mosquitoes transmit a variety of diseases including malaria and yellow fever. Always take prophylactic medicine if visiting a mosquito-prone area.

Disease-carrying insects

Bites from insects can transmit various nasty diseases. The mosquito, which can transmit malaria, dengue (viral infection) and yellow fever, is the most important. Of these, malaria is probably the most widespread health threat to travellers.

Travellers to malaria areas should always take prophylactic medicine. Personal factors and the particular area being visited will determine the most appropriate anti-malaria drug. Get expert advice by consulting a reputable travel advisory clinic. Start taking preventative medication a few days before reaching a malaria area so you can switch medication should you develop side effects. It is important to prevent mosquito bites.

MOSQUITO-BITE PREVENTION

- Avoid camping near swamps and pools of water.
- Always wear long-sleeved shirts and long trousers.
- Wear a netting veil over a brimmed hat.
- Apply an insect repellent to the skin.
- Take extra precautions at sunset and at night when mosquitoes are most active.
- Burn insect-repellent coils and citronella candles in the evening.
- Always keep netting doors of tents zipped up.
- Sleep under a mosquito net.

Blood-borne infections

Hepatitis B and HIV are transmitted by using unsterilized needles and syringes, through blood transfusion and sexual intercourse. An effective hepatitis-B vaccine is available and is recommended.

Take a small supply of injection needles, syringes and drip sets in your first-aid kit in case you are admitted to a Third-World hospital.

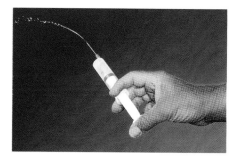

It is better to carry a small supply of syringes, needles and IV equipment when travelling in less developed countries.

FIRST AID

The medical supplies you take along on the trip can vary immensely, depending on the circumstances. The most important consideration is the level of first-aid or medical training available.

Always perform a risk analysis for the proposed trip. Check whether there are any special risks such as altitude, tropical diseases, etc. Include in this planning any special medical problems that an individual may have.

Always consider weight and space when packing a first-aid kit. Choose multifunctional items and keep them all together in an organized waterproof container. Do not include everyday personal medicine in the first-aid kit, which must be kept for emergencies only.

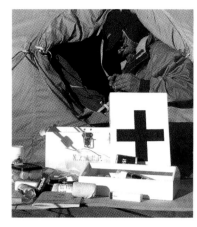

Extensive medical supplies may be necessary if you have to be entirely self-reliant and intend travelling to very remote or desolate regions.

Plan the contents of your first-aid kit carefully according to your group and activity. Always replenish supplies and replace outdated medication beforehand.

POST-TRAUMATIC STRESS DISORDER (PTSD)

This is a common psychological response to an emotionally traumatic event. Many survival situations may lead to PTSD, such as experiencing the death or serious injury of a member of one's group, being involved in the rescue or emergency medical care of someone who is severely injured or who dies, or experiencing a personal life-threatening assault or rape.

Specialized debriefing sessions held soon after the traumatic event and conducted by a trained counsellor are recommended, as they can be helpful.

FIRST-AID KIT FOR SMALL GROUP

The following kit is suitable for a small hiking group going away for about a week to a remote location:

- 2 pairs disposable latex gloves (protection from blood)
- Pocket mask (protection during mouth-to-mouth resuscitation)
- 1 large (300x300mm/12x12in) sterile wound dressing (to cover wounds/stop bleeding)
- 2 small (100x100mm/4x4in) sterile dressings (bleeding & wounds)
- 2 burn dressings e.g. hydrogel (200x200mm/8x8in)
- 1 crepe bandage (+100mm/4in wide) (joint sprains and holding dressings in place)
- 1 small roll adhesive tape
- 1 SAM® splint (fractures)
- Space blanket
- 2 sachets povidine-iodine disinfectant (10ml/$^1/_3$oz)
- Low-reading clinical thermometer (diagnosing fever and hypothermia)
- Scissors and tweezers
- Needle (removing splinters)
- Medication (small quantities)
- Paracetamol – codeine tablets (pain), Acetiminophen (USA)
- Anti-inflammatory drugs e.g. Ibuprofen or aspirin (sprains)
- Antihistamine tablets e.g. Promethazine (allergy and nausea)
- Oil of cloves (toothache)
- Loperamide (diarrhoea)
- Antibiotic e.g. Ciprofloxacin (infection)
- Antifungal ointment
- Saline eye wash (.9 per cent) – 10ml sterile sachet

COMMUNICATION AND INTERACTION

Being seen and rescued is doubtless one of the top survival priorities. Once your ETA (estimated time of arrival) is well past, it is likely that some form of search will be organized, especially if you have left details with friends or family members. If you are not expected for a while, things might take a little longer.

Persuading the authorities to organize and maintain an effective search in an unforeseen emergency is not always easy, especially in Third World countries. The persistent presence of friends and family members and strong political or economic pressure may be necessary to keep organized search attempts active. It is worth priming your friends and family about this 'just in case'.

Red smoke signal flares are effective for attracting attention because they are easily visible, especially at night.

HOW TO BE SEEN

A signal is the best way to alert a search party to your whereabouts. Signalling can take many forms, ranging from the oldest and simplest (mirrors, whistles and fires) to the most modern (radios, mobile phones and transponders). Aim to be imaginative in making visible signs and signals, and make the best use of whatever you have at your disposal, be it pieces of vehicle wreckage or materials found in your environment.

Inset: *Car mirrors are very useful as signalling devices.*

Mirrors

Mirrors are very successful signalling devices. If you do not have one in your survival kit, try to create one by using the base of a cup, pot, or any suitable metal object. Glass bottle bases and car mirrors can also be used as signalling devices. Having a sighting hole in the middle of a mirror will help you locate and aim it better at a rescue craft (i.e. a ship or aeroplane). If there is no hole you should look alongside the mirror. Place your free hand in front of the mirror so that it partly obscures the aeroplane or ship, shift the mirror until the sun's reflection is on your hand before removing the hand. Remember to move the mirror in slow arcs to make sure the flash it emits is seen properly.

Any flattish shiny object can be used to reflect the sun.

Signal fires

- Arrange three fires in a triangle at equal distances apart.
- If you are confident that searchers will be out looking for you or suspect you are close to an aeroplane or shipping lane, then pre-arrange the three fires so they can be lit quickly and easily.
- The triangle of fires should be set up to ensure they will give plenty of light at night or produce plenty of smoke in the daytime.
- If there is enough fuel available, keep at least one fire burning permanently.
- Green branches or vehicle tyres give good, dense smoke; chop them into small pieces to produce black smoke.
- Pick your site for maximum visibility.
- If you are near water, bear in mind that fires made on small rafts and positioned in the middle of streams or ponds in an area with few clearings have been sufficient to alert rescuers.

- Material that contrasts with the background is useful to make ground-to-air signalling more visible.
- The larger your material, the better.
- A cross, triangle or an SOS pattern (Save Our Souls . . . – – – . . .) are sure to attract attention.
- Successful rescue methods survivors have used include controlled burning of bush patches; logs and stones laid in a pattern; and even diverting a small stream to make ponds that resemble an SOS signal.

A selection of rescue flares and equipment

This waterproof flashing strobe light is effective for signalling as it is bright enough to attract attention over a long distance, particularly at night.

Lamplight

Lamplight is highly visible at night and is a valuable way of signalling from mountaintops, cliff faces, boats and islands. Three repeated flashes or the SOS signal are universally acknowledged distress signals. (The International Mountain Distress Signal entails sending six flashes a minute, followed by a minute's wait and then repeated.)

Avoid cross-threading when screwing a mini flare into its firing apparatus.

Flares

Flares are by far the most effective signalling devices. While any flare will attract attention, red is regarded as the most visible colour. Use flares sparingly and only when you are almost certain they will be noticed. Remember that in any search effort, searchers will probably be looking in a 360° arc. As there is no guarantee that searchers will be looking your way, it might be necessary to fire several flares in quick succession to ensure you are visible. There is a fair variety of commercial flares available. If you select one that fires from a pistol (the Very flare), ensure that you load it correctly – the brass cartridge should be pointing towards the firing pin. Mini flares (including small flare pens) require you to first screw the flare in, then pull a trigger lever back against a spring. On releasing this, the flare fires.

All hand-held flares should be held above the head, well away from your face on the downwind side of your body and craft. Since all flares can become hot during use, be careful when handling them, particularly if you are in a rubber raft or wooden craft.

Radio communication

Most small boats and all aeroplanes are fitted with two-way radio systems. Radio is the best way to communicate if you have power and the set is still in working order. If possible send a 'Mayday' (French: m'aidez – help me) or an SOS message before you crash (if in a craft) or are stranded. When the radio set is on and tuned properly, transmission usually takes place by simply pushing a button on the hand-held microphone. If distortion, a weak signal or low battery power prevent you from transmitting a clear voice message, use the button to send an SOS in Morse code: short-short-short-long-long-long-short-short-short.

Many batteries are less effective when they are very cold. If you have small sealed batteries, try heating them against your body. Never warm batteries on a fire.

Modern boats are often fitted with a rescue transponder that sends out signals. These are linked to SatNav (Satellite Navigation) systems that indicate the precise position. A transponder should always be switched on as soon as you find yourself in serious trouble.

RADIO SET CHECKLIST

Although some radio sets have very complex electronics, always check the following important aspects:

- **Power** Is it connected to batteries? Do the batteries still work? If not, do you have replacement batteries or do you have a generator or similar device to recharge the existing batteries?
- **Radio set** Is it fully switched on? Check power lights and listen for any sort of hum.
- **Transmit button** Look for a type of 'transmit' switch or button.
- **Tuning dial** Turn the dial through every frequency. If you hear conversation, cut across it immediately with your distress call. On VHF (very high frequency) radios, Channel 16 is usually used for distress channel messages.
- **Line of sight** A VHF transmitter may only be able to transmit signals within line of sight. If this becomes apparent, rather wait until you can see a search aeroplane or boat before wasting scarce power.

A prominent sign such as this SOS made of stones can attract attention and alert rescuers to your position.

GIVING YOUR POSITION TO SEARCHERS

If you know where you are on a map or you know precisely where you are heading to and want to communicate your exact position to searchers, you need to
use a set of coordinates to set out your SOS message. A system of six-figure
coordinates is usually used in this type of message. Example: SOS 157628
(• indicates dot, short = indicates dash and long | indicates pause)

S	O	S	1	5	7	6	2	8
•••	= = =	•••	• = = =	•••••	= = •••	= ••••	•• = =	= = = ••

This system is useful if you are using a lamp to signal an aircraft while moving, or
if you are only able to communicate via Morse code due to poor signal conditions.

Try to preserve all possible battery power for emergencies or for signalling
when you see a search vehicle or aeroplane. You might need to disconnect the
battery if a radio set is permanently 'live' (some larger craft have this capability). Keep the batteries warm – place them in a sleeping bag or close to your
body (beware of acid from leaking lead-acid batteries).

Limit distress calls by keeping them short and establish regular call times (i.e.
every two hours): even if searchers are only picking up your call signals at the
limit of their frequency range, they will know when to anticipate your call in
order to trace it more accurately.

Cellular phone communication

Cellular (mobile) phones have an emergency frequency that transmits at a higher intensity than voice mes-sages. If you have a cellular signal, try sending a message by dialling the emergency number of your service provider. Another option is to send a short text SMS (short messaging service) distress mes-sage via your cellu-lar (mobile) phone. If neither method is successful, try turning your cell-phone on and off in an SOS pattern.

Try your cellular phone briefly at various times of the day as the range can vary according to atmospheric conditions.

You might be heard by one of the military or civilian 'ears in the sky', which monitor all signals from most parts of the earth. Short Morse code-like signals are the easiest to separate from other background electronic 'noise'. It might take a day or two before your distress message is analyzed, but it might be your pathway to rescue. If you have the means, try sending an SOS and a 6-figure grid reference via radio, cellphone or transponder.

Infrared traces

Huddling together in freezing conditions does more than share warmth between group members and reduce individual heat loss; it also creates a large infrared (heat) trace. By using infrared radar devices and goggles, civilian and military sources are able to detect people on the ground. A large heat trace is more visible than smaller individual traces.

A larger infrared (heat) trace is given off by a large, tight-knit group, which is more easily detectable than that emitted by an individual.

ORGANIZED SEARCHES

Knowledge of search procedures is useful if you are lost as it enables you to anticipate rescuers' methods. For example, shout only during the 'listening' times, i.e. the period just after you hear the search party's calls.

An example of a patterned search.

In all searches, the group members should stop and whistle or call every two minutes, then listen for 30 seconds without moving before calling again. This time gap applies to very difficult uneven terrain; however, it may vary up to five minutes on flat, open terrain. If there are several search parties, you should synchronize watches or else all you might 'find' is the other search party.

If it is possible to conduct a hasty search without jeopardizing the safety of the rest of your group or getting yourself into difficulties, then a preliminary search should be attempted before calling for outside help. The sooner you start a preliminary search the better, because the search area often widens rapidly as time passes and the victim wanders further off.

Hasty searches

As soon as you discover someone is missing, you should organize a hasty search. Using whatever knowledge you can glean quickly, you can establish whether to search back along the line of your original route or to one or the other side. Return to the last known position of the missing person. Look for places where the subject could have diverted from the route. Call loudly and regularly but remember to listen between calls. Be careful not to destroy valuable clues that could you lead you to the subject.

SEARCHING IN A NUTSHELL

- Get all the information.
- Plan the search.
- Confine the subject.
- Search for clues.

SEARCH PLANNING

If your hasty search fails, you should act immediately. If possible, get help from a search and rescue team. An experienced search team will have access to trained and equipped ground searchers, vehicles, radio communications, aircraft and tracker dogs. Above all, they should have an experienced search management capability. If you are unable to get immediate help, it is up to you and your group to do the searching.

How to start search planning

- The last known position of the patient is the starting point for most search planning; decide in consultation with the group which areas to search.
- Use a map if you have one.
- If the group is big enough, split into self-sufficient search teams, make sure that each team has a specific task to perform or area to search.
- Tasks should be completed within an agreed time period, after which the team must return to your base to report back.
- Cover natural hazards and places a person would walk through.
- Only do intensive patterned searches as a last resort if the subject is likely to be unresponsive and well hidden.
- Hunt for clues (footprints, damaged vegetation, etc.) as the search area is narrowed down.

Apart from physically searching for the missing person, other techniques can be used to find a mobile person.

- Place cut-offs or lookouts that will detect the person moving out of the area you are searching.
- Try to attract the missing person to you, using regular blasts of a car horn, a light in a prominent position that can be safely approached at night, or a line of arrows in the sand directing the person to safety.
- Leave notes in sheltered places that the subject may visit.
- Do not jeopardize the group's safety.

A search team, including a specially trained dog, has been dropped off by a rescue helicopter. Dogs are extremely effective in locating avalanche victims.

PLANNING TIPS & CHECK LIST

When planning a search, ensure you have all the necessary information to conduct a successful operation.

- Carefully plan and control your search. Haphazard searching wastes time and resources, and destroys the clues.
- Gather all available information on the missing person and the circumstances of the incident.
- Try to put yourself in the position of the missing person – think of various scenarios that could have led to the situation.
- Establish a missing person's likely behaviour pattern.
- Small children tend not to go far but may become frightened and hide. They could crawl into a concealed place and fall asleep. They may not necessarily respond to their name being called.
- Hikers tend to travel long distances and prefer to stick to paths. If they miss the trail they may blunder on, hoping to make their way back on to familiar territory.
- Emotionally distressed people may seek out a quiet place or avoid searchers.

VITAL INFORMATION NEEDED

- Last known position.
- Intentions and direction of travel.
- Experience and knowledge of the area.
- Full description – physical and clothing.
- List of items in the person's possession.
- Shoe sole pattern.
- Cigarette brand, sweet wrappers.
- Signalling capability (light source, whistle).
- Locations the person(s) could head for.
- Interpersonal conflict prior to the incident.
- Medical/mental problems and emotional state.

PROCEDURES WITH RESCUE CRAFT

Sea rescues can take place in open water or from boats with varying levels of sea-worthiness. Rescue craft vary from small boats to large vessels and helicopters. In many cases the water is rough with large waves or swells. This could make it difficult for the rescue craft to approach your vessel, particularly if it has loose spars or masts that can cause damage. You may be signalled to jump into the open water. This might seem daunting, but be guided by the expertise of the rescuers and follow their instructions.

- Ensure that you are wearing a life jacket and that it is fastened before moving into the water.
- If there are several people being rescued, try to stay linked together.

- If being picked up from a boat by another craft, stand at the rail on the lee side (away from the direction from which the wind is blowing) until the other craft draws alongside. Then quickly climb over your rail and try to grasp the rail or ladder of the other craft before releasing your grip.
- Jumping the gap should be seen as a last resort.
- A group should not swamp the rescue boat by frantically jumping or climbing onto it all at once.
- It is vital that one person takes command to avoid panic and coordinate actions of the people being rescued.
- Although difficult to climb, ladders or nets are often used to rescue someone from rough waters.

A hypothermic surfer is pulled onto a hastily organized rescue vessel in choppy waters.

Helicopter rescues

Although aircraft are frequently used as spotters, helicopters are usually used for final rescue operations. They do, however, have limitations. They require an obstruction-free entrance and exit path, and cannot touch down if the slope is too steep as their blades will hit the slope (see precautions, pp180–81). Even turbojet helicopters have less control at high altitude levels.

When guiding a landing helicopter, face it with your back to the wind and both arms pointing forward.

HOW TO ASSIST RESCUERS

If you are part of a group that is lost, it is essential to assist searchers by leaving clues on your whereabouts and movements. This can be done by stopping to build cairns, making ground markers with your initials and an arrow to show direction of movement, as well as cutting arrows into trees or bending twigs. If you are sheltering somewhere such as a deep cave, you should leave markers at the entrance. You cannot afford to miss the calls of the searchers when they pass nearby and you are possibly asleep or unconscious.

A smoke flare is being used to guide an RAF (Royal Air Force) helicopter to a landing zone during one of its frequent and indispensable training exercises for rescue personnel.

CHOOSING A LANDING ZONE

It is important to choose the landing zone carefully. For safety reasons, pilots prefer not to lower vertically into a clearing, but aim instead for a low-level horizontal approach, usually landing into the wind.

- A landing zone requires a clearing of firm, flat ground with a slope of less than 10° and at least 30m (100ft) in diameter.
- The site should have no high surrounding obstructions such as high trees or large rocks, to allow for approach and take-off at an angle.
- In particular, avoid being anywhere near telephone or power cables as these may be difficult to see from the air and can be fatal to the air crew.
- Clear the landing surface of small, light objects such as twigs, branches and even gravel if possible. If in a snow-covered area, try to compact the snow to make it easier for the pilot to land.
- Give a wind indication – this can be done by using a windsock, a smoke indicator, a large T with the top of the T placed upwind or an appropriate hand signal (i.e. face with your back to the wind, both arms pointing forward – see photo far left).
- You can assist the helicopter crew in locating you by flashing a mirror or lamp, setting off smoke or other flares or waving brightly coloured clothing (see below). It is helpful to mark the touchdown point with a large H-sign scratched into the soil or made of inlaid rocks packed together (see illustration p180).

PRECAUTIONS AROUND HELICOPTERS

Working around helicopters can be very dangerous because the noise and downdraft caused by the rotors disorient people and make it impossible to shout instructions. The spinning blades of a helicopter's main and tail rotors are invisible and they can easily decapitate the unwary.

- Note that you should always approach the aircraft from the front or side, NEVER from the rear.
- Only approach AFTER you have been clearly signalled to do so by the pilot or engineer.
- Once the pilot decides to shut down the engine, wait until the blades have totally stopped spinning before approaching – many rotor blades 'droop' or drop close to the ground as they slow down.
- If the helicopter has touched down on a slope, never approach or leave a helicopter on the uphill side. This will ensure that you avoid the blades, which can spin very close to the ground on the rising slope.
- As you move towards the helicopter, crouch down and do not have any loose articles on you (i.e. hats, sleeping bags or ropes).
- Beware of holding long items vertically (e.g. folded stretchers).
- If it is impractical or difficult for the helicopter to land, the pilot may hover with one wheel on the ground, or use a cable winch to lower rescue personnel, lift a stretcher carrying a patient, or perform a sea rescue.

Assist the pilot by demarcating a suitable, cleared touchdown point with a large, visible H-sign.

- The winch sling can carry a massive electrical (static) charge from the aircraft, so always allow the winch to ground or touch water before grabbing it.
- NEVER fasten the winch to a solid object (i.e. a yacht, tree or a stretcher) until requested to because the helicopter may have to break away at any stage.
- If you are wearing a climbing harness, you can simply clip in with a carabiner to the strop (rope or metal band around a block for support) or to both strop shackles.
- If you are using the lifting strop, raise your arms, slip the strop over them, fasten the grommet (if it has one) and tuck it under your armpits.
- Give a thumbs-up signal before you link your hands. DO NOT raise your arms again after giving this signal.

Emergency flares fired from two distressed boats light up the night sky to show their position.

- If being lifted off a small projection such as a rock platform, wait below the level of the platform or lie flat until the helicopter skid or wheel touches the ground. Thereafter, approach the helicopter door as instructed by the flight engineer.
- On reaching the cabin, allow the winchman to turn you and pull you in. Follow his instructions carefully.

GLOSSARY

Abseil To descend a steep drop by sliding in a controlled fashion down a rope that is passed around the body or through a mechanical device to increase friction.

Altimeter Mechanical or electrical device used to measure height above sea level, normally by reference to surrounding air pressure, which falls with increasing altitude (see also GPS for electronic altitude measurement).

AVPU Scale (Level of consciousness) A- Alert; V- responds to Verbal stimuli (i.e. talking); P- responds only to Painful stimuli (e.g. a pin prick); U- Unresponsive.

Belaying Holding the rope attached to the climber in such a way to stop a fall. Mechanical 'belay devices' or rope friction around the belayer's body or a suitable projection are usual methods.

Carabiner A metal snap-ring that can open on one side (the gate). Used to attach ropes or slings to pieces of climbing equipment.

Celestial navigation Finding one's way across the earth's surface using stars as navigational aids.

Compass A device that indicates magnetic north, usually by means of a swinging magnetized needle. (See GPS for electronic alternatives).

CPR Cardiopulmonary resuscitation. A combination of mouth-to-mouth respiration with external cardiac massage.

Crampons Metal frames with down- and front-pointing spikes fitted to mountaineering boots to assist one's passage on hard ice or snow.

Crevasse A large and sometimes deep split in the surface of a glacier, often hidden under overlying snow cover.

Distillation The splitting off by evaporation of a liquid at a certain boiling point from a mixture of fluids. Also used to refer to purifying water by evaporating it from a mixture of water and impurities in some form of distillation apparatus.

Filter feeders Small aquatic animals that obtain food by straining large quantities of water through gills or other food-collecting organs.

Frostbite Low-temperature condition in which the water inside body cells freezes, which can rupture the cell walls and internal organelles. The nature of the damage becomes apparent when the body tissue thaws.

Glacier A 'river' of frozen ice lying in a valley that is usually steep. Glaciers tend to'creep' downhill under the effect of gravity and the increased weight of fresh snowfall found on the upper reaches.

GPS Global Positioning System – a sophisticated electronic device used for navigation that exchanges signals with a series of fixed-position satellites in order to triangulate its 3-dimensional position on the earth. GPS devices are able to provide coordinates, altitude readings, compass bearings and track travel.

Grid North The direction of north given on a map with reference to an accepted convention of N–S and E–W lines for that specific area.

Harness A specialized safety belt that

fastens around the legs and body; used in rock climbing and related activities.

HIV Human Immuno-deficiency Virus. Associated with and thought to be responsible for AIDS (Acquired Immune Deficiency Syndrome).

Hypothermia A serious condition asso ciated with exposure to low tempera tures and wind chill. The body systemat ically shuts down certain functions as a protective mechanism to preserve its core temperature as long as possible.

Infrared (radiation) Electromagnetic radiation below the visible red spectrum. This is conventionally registered and referred to as 'heat'.

Karrimat A generic term for a closed-cell (dense) foam mattress.

Lee side The side of a craft away from the force of the wind (downwind).

LZ Landing Zone – a specific area desig nated for helicopter landing and take off.

Magnetic declination The amount by which the direction of true north differs from that of magnetic north on a partic ular section of the earth's surface.

Magnetic North The point on the Northern Hemisphere of the earth's sur face that corresponds to the conver gence of the electro-magnetic lines of force surrounding the earth. Located by means of a compass. This point is NOT at the geographical (rotational) North pole.

Near-drowning Cessation of breathing and possibly cardiac function as a result of immersion in water. Often incorrectly referred to as 'drowning'. The latter term is used medically to refer to someone who has died as a result of immersion in water.

Quinze A dome-shaped igloo .

SatNav Satellite Navigation (see GPS).

Scree slope A slope covered with many small, loose rocks or boulders, making for unstable footing.

Snare An animal trap made from a wire or cord noose.

Strop (winch) The broad loop found attached to the end of a rescue rope or cable, into which the victim places his or her upper body in order to be lifted.

Topography The landform of an area.

Transponder A device that sends a sig nal which can be picked up by a suitable (often satellite-based) receiver to assist in locating a group in difficulties, such as an avalanche transponder or a yacht transponder.

Triage The process of determining the priority in which victims should receive medical treatment or be evacuated according to their long-term survival chances. Although there are internation ally recognized formats for triage, com mon sense may have to dictate in some emergency situations.

True North The geographical North Pole (established as the point of rotation of the earth around its axis).

UV radiation Electromagnetic radiation that occurs beyond the upper (blue) vis ible spectrum. UV radiation is harmful to living tissue, particularly in high doses or for prolonged periods of time. 'Sunburn' is caused by UV rays.

VHF (radio) Very High Frequency radio, also called 'short wave'. It has a much longer range than conventional radio as it 'bounces' signals around the earth by reflecting them from a layer of the atmosphere.

INDEX

INDEX   187

MORSE CODE

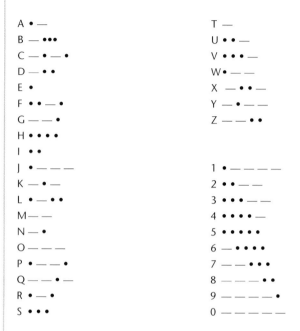

A •—   T —
B —•••   U ••—
C —•—•   V •••—
D —••   W•——
E •   X —••—
F ••—•   Y —•——
G ——•   Z ——••
H ••••
I ••
J •———   1 •————
K —•—   2 ••———
L •—••   3 •••——
M——   4 ••••—
N—•   5 •••••
O———   6 —••••
P •——•   7 ——•••
Q ——•—   8 ———••
R •—•   9 ————•
S •••   0 —————

Leave a gap of a few seconds between letters (depends on your speed) and a bigger one between words.

AAA = END OF SENTENCE   AR = END OF MESSAGE
IMI = Do not understand — repeat   SOS = ••• ——— •••

BODY SIGNALS

PICK US UP

NEED MECHANICAL
HELP

LAND HERE

YES

NO

ALL IS WELL

CAN PROCEED
SHORTLY

HAVE RADIO

DO NOT ATTEMPT
TO LAND HERE

NEED MEDICAL
ASSISTANCE

USE DROP
MESSAGE

GROUND-TO-AIR CODE

I SERIOUS INJURY – IMMEDIATE CASUALTY EVACUATION NEEDED

II NEED MEDICAL SUPPLIES

F NEED FOOD AND WATER

N NEGATIVE (NO)

A AFFIRMATIVE (YES) – 'Y' WILL ALSO BE UNDERSTOOD

LL ALL IS WELL

X UNABLE TO MOVE ON

 AM MOVING ON THIS WAY

K INDICATE DIRECTION TO PROCEED

 DO NOT UNDERSTAND

 NEED COMPASS AND MAP

△ THINK SAFE TO LAND HERE (BROKEN AT ANGLES MEANS ATTEMPTING TAKE-OFF)

 NEED RADIO SIGNAL, LAMP BATTERY

⌐ AIRCRAFT BADLY DAMAGED

VHF EMERGENCY CHANNEL: 16

INTERNATIONAL
WHISTLE/LIGHT SIGNAL:
6 BLASTS/FLASHES REPEATED

ESSENTIAL SURVIVAL STEPS:
Sit — Think — Observe — Plan
Avoid PANIC and undue HASTE —
take a few deep breaths
before acting

FIRST AID ESSENTIALS:
Hazard, Hello, Help
ABC — Airway, Breathing,
Circulation

LEVEL OF
CONSCIOUSNESS SCALE:
A Alert
V responds to Verbal stimuli
P responds to Pain
U Unresponsive

ESSENTIAL KNOTS AND LASHINGS:

Figure of eight

Clove hitch

Square lashing

Auscape : Main cover pic,22, 24

Cathy O'Dowd Collection : 30(a)

Christel Clear : 158(a-b)

Danja Köhler : 96(b-c)

Dr. Lance Michell : 151, 161(b)

E. Roberts : 137(a)

Ffotograff / Mark Hannaford : 95, 160(a)

Frank Lane Pic Agency / Zingel Eichhorn : 77;

Gallo Images / Getty Images.com : 2-3, 4-5, 6, 48, 52(b), 62, 74, 86, 100, 124, 161(a), 162(a);

Hedgehog House / Barbara Brown : 128(b),

Hedgehog House / Colin Monteath : 21, 50, 110(b), 155(a), 156(a),

Hedgehog House / Lydia Bradey : 9(b),

Hedgehog House / Peter Cleary : 181,

Hedgehog House / Rob Brown : 137(b),

Hedgehog House / Walter Fowlie : 179;

Inpra (Sygma) : 13, 60;

Jack Jackson : 20;

Legend Photography / Andy Belcher : 16(b), 117;

Lochman Transparancies / Dennis Sarson : 65(b),

Lochman Transparancies / Jiri Lochman : 94;

Martyn Farr : 163(a);

Mountain Camera / John Cleare : 122, 135, 141, 143, 155(b), 157, 164(b), 166, 175, 178(a);

NHIL / Anthony Johnson : 38(a-b);

NHIL / Clinton Whaits :15(a), 134(d);

NHIL / Jacques Marais : Front cover (tr & br), Back cover, 8, 9(a), 10, 11, 12(a), 12(b), 14, 16(a), 17, 19, 27(a-e), 30(b), 29(a-c), 33(b), 34(a-c), 35, 36(a-c), 37a, 39(a-d), 40, 44, 47, 54(a-b), 55(a),56, 63, 64, 66(a-b). 67(a-b), 68(a), 70, 71(b), 78, 79, 82, 88, 90(a-b), 92, 96(a),99(a-b), 102, 107, 110(a), 119(a-b), 131, 132, 134(a), 136(a-b), 142, 144, 146, 148,149, 150, 153, 154, 156(b), 162(b), 163(b), 168, 169(a-b), 170, 171, 172, 173, 177;

NHIL / Nick Aldridge : 15(b), 32, 33(a), 104

Picture Box : Spine Pic, 112, 55(b)

Photo Access : 65(a), 1

Raytheon Marine Company : 111(a)

Richard Sale : 52(a)

SIL : 37(b), 72(a-b), 109(a), 159, 160(b);

SIL / Juan Espi : 133(a-b), 134(b-c);

SIL / Kelly Walsh : 28;

SIL / Leonard Hoffmann :73(a);

SIL / Mike Carelse : 164(a);

SIL / Nigel J Dennis : 73(b), 81, 109(b);

SIL / Ryno Reyneke : 71(a);

SIL / Shaen Adey : 116,

Stock Shot / D.Willis : 138, 178(b),

Stock Shot / Jess Stock : 114, 118

Travel Ink / David Toase : 41